SNAFU

A Hysterical Memoir About
Why the Government Doesn't Work

ELLEN ROBERGE

ISBN:10: 0615610293

ISBN-13: 978-0615610290 BureauRat Publishing

Dedication

To all those conscientious federal employees
I had the pleasure of working with for 28 years, and to HHH.

Contents

Acknowledgments

My thanks to the Wizard of Id comic strip authors Parker and Hart for their comic strip of December 29, 2002, which so simply and accurately sums up the crux of my entire book.

SO YOU REALLY WANT TO
WORK FOR THE GOVERNMENT?

L isten, be honest, you know how *you* react when someone tells you they work for the Federal Government. People who work for the Government have a reputation of being lazy, recklessly spending your hard earned taxpayer's dollars and they can't be fired. But when I was 22, I had no idea that's how most people felt, and worse, that I would eventually agree with them. I also became quickly familiar with a term, SNAFU (Situation Normal All F***ed Up) which would describe all of the situations in this book to a tee and which I heard someone say almost every day of my career. I want to be clear up front, however, I'm not writing about ALL Government workers – not the friendly, helpful park ranger you may remember fondly from a Grand Canyon trip. I'm writing about all those parts of the military/industrial complex of Government that is primarily shaped by their relationship with big money/big business (mainly defense, Wall Street) that have morphed into something that people instinctively know is a bad sub-set of Government but for which we don't have a name.

I can't say I've known anyone that killed to get a Government job, but that was about the only thing I hadn't seen; unless you counted the vultures waiting to replace dying managers. Once the workforce got wind of a dying manager, the computer keyboards got more action than Tiger Woods, as the resumes were furiously prepared (on the taxpayer's dime, of course). I was grateful to get my first job, working for the Department of the Army on a military installation, but had no idea what working for the Government would come to mean to me. I just knew the Human Resources office was telling me I had a great pension and health benefits.

In the beginning it was just a job. Twenty-eight years later in 2003 when I took early retirement at age 50, I knew it was the best decision I'd ever made. Early retirement was the only way to calm my pounding head, gurgling stomach, and nasty attitude. Once again, as so many times in the past, the Navy had waltzed yet another new software program through the door, claiming it was the panacea to all the woes of the existing legacy systems, and told everyone they had to use it or else. I was tapped to teach classes to the workforce on how to use the new software. Every day for months on end I tried to teach a disgruntled, adversarial group of Government employees who didn't want to be there; and neither did I. Instead of getting a migraine a month, now I was getting one every day. If looks and remarks coming from the trainees were rotten tomatoes, I would've had more than my minimum daily requirement of lycopene.

The Government simply does not work. In an effort to shed its skin like a snake, about a year before I retired, the Department of Defense (DoD) implemented what they called a "rightsizing plan." "Downsizing" had had such a negative connotation and the highly paid consultants they hired advised our Commanding Officer that "rightsizing" was the new politically correct buzz word. Unfortunately, as does much of what the DoD implements, the plan was fouled up. Most of the employees who had been eligible to retire for years who they were hoping would retire were not interested in leaving their cushy Government jobs, even with a

$25,000 cash incentive bonus to go. And, they didn't count on the numbers of employees who were management pets or those who knew where all the bodies were buried who had long ago been promised an early-out with bonus if one was offered. There were only so many to go around and the pets and the would-be whistleblowers got theirs first, before the old slugs they really hoped would go.

I had worked very hard to establish myself as a management pet, since leaving the job I'd held in the Contracting field for over 20 years for a different job as a staffer (management gopher). I had high hopes this staffer position, paid out of the Command's ever shrinking overhead budget, would increase my chances of being offered early retirement. Four years as a staffer finally paid off and I said goodbye to Government.

The Command had also negotiated a deal with Washington to backfill many of the same positions they were eliminating with a simple rewrite of the position description into brand-new jobs. And hopefully, they'd fill those jobs with a fresh, young and enthusiastic group of recent college graduates from the college next door. The college had donated the land to the Government that our building was built on and they had a quid pro quo program established with the Government for hiring their graduates as interns. What I saw, as I worked to train the interns before I retired, were that they were know-it-all young slugs fresh from college with an attitude that spoke volumes that they were the "entitled" generation. It didn't take long for me to learn that a young cocky slug was worse than an old "I don't give a shit" slug. Once again, the Government ignored all the warning signs of this young blood's lack of willingness to compromise, work under time constraints, arrive to work on time, not disappear without letting the boss know where they were going, not call in sick regularly, and most importantly, not back talk. What the Government failed to recognize until too late is they were truly a different generation from baby-boomers and despite the baby-boomers advice to management to terminate the bad seeds during their "career conditional" status, they started promoting them in droves beyond their levels of competence faster than you can say "Jack Rabbit."

So, I left the sinking ship still full of old bureaurats and increasing numbers of "I deserve the best" young bureaurats. Even with a 10% penalty to my annual pension because I got out five years early, it was still a sweet deal. Even though I would later work for the DoD as a independent consultant I also discovered there was no difference working for a DoD contractor than there was working the DoD, except you could be fired or you could quit and take your 401K with you. Long before I retired, when I tried to tell my DoD bosses that something was stupid, and recommended a smarter, faster, cheaper way to do it, I'd only wind up being told to do it the way I was told. My only alternative would have been to quit and receive only what I had paid in to my pension, which was not enough to live on for more than a year. As an independent consultant, I experienced exactly the same situations, except this time I wasn't bound by the golden handcuffs of my lifetime Government pension that I would give up if I quit, so I refused to do it the stupid, expensive way and quit, twice. I was, after all, still a taxpayer, but now I had my Government pension to fall back on, which made me feel powerful for the first time in my life. Powerful maybe, but when I decided I wanted to work as a consultant again, what I'd learn was the DoD contractors didn't want to rock the boat with the Government and when the Government told them they had a "do not hire" list that was updated regularly and given to the DoD contractors, my name was on the list.

For most highly paid Government employees, if they worked until they were eligible to retire they could possibly look forward to a pension that could be as much as $75,000 a year, depending, of course, in how skilled they'd been at bullshitting, backstabbing, ass kissing and promoting the incompetent to the same high levels of Government they'd achieved. I had decided long ago I wanted nothing to do with being in management. I knew I'd drive myself and my employees crazy by trying to get them to work, and except for a shining few I'd met throughout my career, I knew it would be like teaching a pig to sing; it annoys the pig, and it just doesn't work. That didn't mean I didn't learn the fine art of ass kissing early on. Ass kissing is the one thing everyone in the Government learns quickly and does well. You won't get very far in Government trying to tell the emperor he's wearing no clothes. As one of my mentors told me, "You can think it, but you can't say it."

I took the civil service exam in 1973, in the hopes of being qualified for a Clerk-Stenographer position, since I'd taken short-hand and typing in high school. I received notification that I had qualified for that position, however, no positions were currently available and my name would be kept on a list and as positions became available, they would contact me. The wheels of Government turn very slowly. Almost a year later, I was contacted and told there were various positions available, and I could call and schedule an interview.

Since it had been some time since I had practiced stenography (I never actually had taken stenography in a work environment), I was actually concerned that I wouldn't measure up, so I sent a letter to the office that wanted to hire me, requesting my status be downgraded from a Clerk Stenographer to a Clerk Typist/Receptionist. And they did exactly that. At the time, I was relieved. Later, knowing what I would come to know about management and many of my co-workers, I would laugh at myself for actually having requested something the Human Resources Office had probably never been asked to do before.

So, I was hired as a Receptionist in a military-run Optometry Clinic on an Army installation in Georgia, which provided optometry services to all the military members stationed there. Since I had only worked very briefly, and married the first man I ever dated, I had not been around a lot of men, military or otherwise. What I learned very quickly was that they have a lot of what I didn't even know at the time was called testosterone. Much later, Tailhook would unfortunately demonstrate this to the world, but this was long before Tailhook. And, frankly, everyone knows that stuff had been going on forever anyway, it had just never made the news. After all was said and done, I also discovered that we live in quite a hypocritical world. Isn't that exactly the kind of person they hire (and consistently reward) to get the job done?

I was the "meet and greet" receptionist in the clinic and also answered the phone and made appointments. One anonymous male military patient started calling me regularly at work, telling me how he'd like to get together with me. He wouldn't tell me who he was and gave no hints about which doctor he saw (there were four military optometrists). In the beginning, I just laughed it off and ended the conversation politely. Then I started asking him not to call me. When none of that seemed to faze him, I reminded him he was calling an official military phone. Nothing seemed to work. At this point, I got scared and told him I was going to call the military police. He persisted. My boss, LTC Abel Adams started noticing how I seemed to be slamming down his official phone on occasion, and called me in to his office to discuss what was going on. When I told him, he called in the Army's Criminal Investigative Division (CID) since it was involving an official military office and phone. Not to be ungrateful, but this was no Crime Scene Investigation group and the guys I dealt with were no Horatio Cane. When the CID guys simply told me the next time the guy called to tell him I'd changed my mind and wanted to get together with him after all, I hesitated and tried not to be too much of a know-it-all when I asked, "Don't you think the guy might be just a little suspicious if I suddenly change my mind now?" I was a little concerned, but I was dealing with the CID after all, surely they wouldn't do anything to endanger my safety? Their attitude was all I had to do was use my wily feminine ways, make a date with him, and they'd take care of everything else. So, as predicted, my stalker bought my sudden change of heart when I told him I had changed my mind because I admired his persistence. I was at least relieved that he was somewhat concerned at first and wanted to know if this wasn't some kind of a trap and if my husband was actually going to meet him. Luckily for me, with my newfound sweet-talking persuasion I didn't even know I possessed, a date was made. I was glad that at least the CID didn't suggest meeting him at the on-base apartment I shared with my husband. By the time my husband received a transfer to another military installation (unrelated to this incident), I was 23, been through a formal CID investigation, including wire-tapping and a "sting" operation, using little ole' me as the bait. Fortunately for me, not much happened, other than having the bejesus scared out of me, but not by my stalker. When he approached me at our agreed to meeting spot in the parking lot, there were so many undercover CID guys that came running toward us, *they* scared me worse than he did. It was a circus and nothing ever came of it for reasons never shared with me. My stalker was confined to his barracks for a night or two and that was that. This was my first SNAFU.

Being a military-wife, I was almost guaranteed a position at my husband's next duty station, wherever it would be. This time I was hired as a Clerk Typist, and was eventually promoted to a Communications Clerk on a Navy base. I had a sweet young Lieutenant Junior Grade (LTJG) for my supervisor, and a salty, fatherly Master Chief Petty Officer who knew everything the LTJG didn't even know he didn't know. It wasn't long before the resident first floor womanizer, Petty Officer Jake Jackson, discovered I was working in the basement. I was receiving uninvited visits from Jake on a daily if not hourly basis. It seemed I was doomed for yet another sting operation, but fortunately Jake took no for an answer, with some encouragement from the fatherly Master Chief. My education in military rules and regulations were constantly being expanded. I came to find out the Commanding Officer's civilian secretary was having an affair with one of the Warrant Officers that worked there. You see, military commissioned and warrant officers face possible court martial for fraternization with enlisted military members of the opposite sex, but not with civilians.

I had also made fast friends with Christa Cummings, a young, good-looking, single civilian woman that worked on the main floor up the steep stairs from the basement. Christa wore the shortest dresses and had the largest (real) breasts of any woman I had ever seen. The guys that worked in the basement knew exactly what time she came down the stairs to pick up her mail. They'd all come out of their basement offices and gather at the bottom of the staircase, waiting for Christa. Christa never disappointed. She ate the attention up. Christa never wanted to get married, she liked "playing the field" and the field was always full of players. Among other things, I overheard one guy saying to another one day as Christa walked away from them that it looked like there were two small puppies fighting underneath her dress. That's exactly the kind of reaction Christa was looking for.

THE DIRTY LITTLE SECRET.

My husband got out of the military, and we eventually settled in central Florida, and I again applied for yet another civil service job at another Navy base, but working for the Army again, but this time for the DoD. The Army was a tenant command and was just renting the space from the Navy. I was hired as a temporary Clerk-Typist, which soon turned into a permanent position. I would go through the next 25 years learning more and more about the true nature of what it meant to work for Uncle Sam.

I worked in one of the many converted WWII barracks buildings on the Navy base, in which the bathroom and water fountain were shut down more than once by Occupational Safety and Health Administration for unsanitary conditions. But the rest of the surroundings were paradise! Not far from my building was one of many beautiful lakes where I never missed the yearly office picnic, where they actually used to serve beer during the picnic. Turns out that probably wasn't the best of ideas since it simply enabled all the alcoholics. One of them would always get drunk and wind up telling the Commanding Officer off, before someone had to come and drag them away. After that incident, our picnics became strictly non-alcoholic (except for the coolers full of beer that were inevitably smuggled in). Back in 1978 there were only a few shopping malls in the area, and the Navy base was located near one of them. There were lots of great restaurants and bars nearby too, since they had a built in military clientele. All great places to disappear in the middle of the work day too, or for just a long, long lunch. This was in the hay day of retirement/going away luncheons that always turned into drunken parties where the majority of the attendees never made it back to work and nothing was ever said or done about it.

In spite of these glory days, the Navy base would later be closed as a result of the Base Realignment and Closure (BRAC) process. This was one of the first times I would begin to understand how politically corrupt everything was in Government, especially the BRAC process. No one could understand why they had calculated that it would cost less money to have young Navy recruits train in the snow and live on the broken down Great Lakes Navy base in Michigan, rather than Florida! Perhaps it had something to do with the persistent circulating rumor that we were working on what had been a hazardous waste site, not to mention the upper level of the building was said to be full of asbestos in the attic? I would always believe the asbestos in the attic resulted in the many future cancer-related illnesses and deaths among my fellow employees that worked in that part of the building. I was lucky; I didn't work in "the asbestos suite." Then, it dawned on me one day. Maybe it had more to do with the commercial value of the Navy base land which would be available for local real estate development once the Navy base was demolished. The local developers started swarming like termites. After much gnashing of teeth, one lucky developer won the bid to clean up the hazardous waste site and build a highly-exclusive, extremely expensive housing development on the former Navy base that was touted to have a real old-fashioned downtown feel. Once completed it bore a strong resemblance to Disney World and it seemed filled with sets from Disney movies.

I worked for Jerry Jeremy's DoD Contracting branch. Jerry was a suave, debonair, sweet-talking, swaggering southern man, who fancied the ladies. He was a first-time newlywed in his 40s. That should have tipped me off, but I hadn't learned that lesson, yet.

This was also my first experience at actually having to work together with another civil servant who was paid the same, and was supposed to do the same work that I did. It was called a typing pool. Remember, this was pre-computers. There were about eight other higher paid civil servants that we supported, and the two of us would type their handwritten rough drafts that they placed in a communal metal military box located on the desk of a retired Navy yeoman, who had gone on to his second career as a civilian Lead Contracting Clerk. We were supposed to go to the Lead Contracting Clerk's desk and take from the box on a first-in, first out basis and then return a typed product to the author(s). Generally, no minimum amount of time to complete the job was ever required, until things started piling up. Then everyone would paperclip a small piece of pink paper they tore off a Government issued pad with "URGENT" printed on it in big black letters. Urgent was never actually defined for me, but when pink is all I could see in the box, I knew it meant Diane Duncan had been disappearing and/or calling in sick again. Diane called in sick a lot, another great ploy that was often used by malingering civil servants. Even when Diane was there, no one seemed to notice that I was the only one making regular visits to the typing pool box, least of all Jerry Jeremy, who was supervisor to both of us. The Lead Contracting Clerk knew, but he wasn't our supervisor. I really started to wonder what was going on, otherwise, why wouldn't they fire Diane for poor performance? When I started complaining to the higher paid civil servants I supported about Diane not carrying her fair share of the workload they just nodded in agreement and told me maybe she'd move on soon and take another Government job somewhere else. I was really baffled by what that meant . . . but not for long.

Let's face it, all the work was getting done (by me), what did anyone (except me) have to complain about? And, as it turned out, Diane Duncan did soon take a job elsewhere, and I learned Jerry Jeremy gave her a glowing recommendation when the Government office she'd applied to called him and asked him if she was a good worker! That's what everyone meant about her moving and taking another job somewhere else. Always, always, perpetuate the lie about the high level of competence of your employees you want to get rid of.

That's the only way most DoD civilian supervisors dealt with employees who didn't work and at the same time, kept their best workers; they encouraged only the deadbeat ones to take jobs elsewhere by giving them a fantastic job recommendation. Because, after all, a DoD supervisor can't be fired either, and none of them want to be bothered by having to follow the mile high stack of civilian personnel regulations in order to comply with what it *still* takes to document and fire a civil servant to this day. The only time in my career that I actually saw an employee fired was for gross fraud, like falsifying a time card or a travel voucher or giving proprietary contractual information to a DoD contractor's competitor. The rest were allowed to be non-performers until they reached the minimum eligibility requirements for retirement, and then they were strongly encouraged to retire. Doesn't mean they did. There were some real dinosaurs roaming around, particularly in upper management. I saw a few truly bad performers (mainly alcoholics) who were only a few years from retirement eligibility who would be allowed to take what is called a Discontinued Service Retirement and retire before they were eligible and start drawing their pension early, most of the time without a penalty to their pension. That was the only way they could get rid of them. And, since all the deadbeat civil servants that I would ever work with had discovered this well known fact as soon as they started working for the Government, they were all model employees until they achieved career status (think tenure for teachers), which was three years. Once they were no longer in a Career Conditional status, they were untouchable and they knew it. Pretty good gig if you could get it.

REALITY BITES.

Jerry Jeremy encouraged me to consider advancing from the secretarial series into what was called the professional series, through a program called the Upward Mobility Program (UMP). The UMP program was established prior to the 1991 requirements implemented by the Defense Acquisition Workforce Improvement Act (DAWIA) which required all Contracting series personnel to have at least 24 hours of college business credits before they could be hired. The UMP was based on the employee's potential to learn professional Government Contracting without having been to college. I would also still be working for Jerry, so this was one of those rare occasions where he could promote an employee and keep them working for him at the same time. I had also made friends with another single female, Janet Jenkins, who was a 40-something, tough-talking professional series Contract Specialist with a master's degree in Contracting, which was almost unheard of back then. The fact that it was from a college no one had even heard of didn't seem to matter. Janet also encouraged me to move into the professional series. There was a definite caste system in Government in those days (and still is frankly) not only in the Government. This was back before the term "political correctness" had ever been used, and if you were a Government secretary you weren't considered a professional. They called it Secretary's Day back then, not Administrative Professionals Day, like they do today. More than once I would hear one of the guys Janet worked with refer to her as a feminazi, among other things. Janet referred to herself as assertive, a word you were beginning to hear a lot in the 80s. The truth was, if you were a tough, smart, assertive woman, you were called a feminazi, or worse, and promotions into top management were hard to come by. However, if you were a tough, assertive guy (and not necessarily smart) you were usually promoted as soon as you applied for the job.

I took everyone's advice, and after competing with many other non-professionals I became a professional Contract Specialist trainee in 1981. Talk about being in the right place at the right time. With the trainee position also came the guarantee for automatic promotions to the next higher pay grade without further competition, as long as you maintained a satisfactory performance rating. I went through a divorce during this time too, which would now made the job even more important to keep, no matter how much bullshit was already starting to pile up.

I would spend the majority of my career as a Contract Specialist. The Contracting Department primarily supported the Program Management Department. Program Managers (PMs) were rewarded (with cash bonuses) for how quickly they got the Contracting Department to award a Government contract to a DoD contractor, no matter how bad the Government specifications were and no matter what the price. PMs didn't care for the Contracting types since it was one of a series of checks and balances supposedly put in place to avoid awarding a contract to an unqualified contractor just because the PM was trying to make his bonus. Contracting folks were mostly referred to as "obstructionists" or "contracts weenies." The other problem was the PMs considered what they did was "real work" and what Contracting did was secretarial work, even though I was officially in the professional series now, just like they were. They considered they were no different from the soldiers, sailors and Marines that actually go to war to defend our country, simply by the fact it was their job to facilitate the purchase of training for the various military departments. I, however, knew a paper pusher is a paper pusher, is a paper pusher; a civil servant ain't a soldier, sailor or Marine. Now granted, some of these PMs were, in fact, also members of the military. But to be a military man or woman basically doing a civil servants' job is usually only temporary and is sometimes required to balance out the numbers of military and civilians at DoD activities.

So now I was a professional contract weenie in training. I was assigned to shadow other Contract Specialists and do their hand prepared negotiation spreadsheets for them. (This was back in the day when a wide yellow tablet of specially lined paper and a pencil were used to prepare the Government's negotiation position.) Imagine my surprise when I attended my first official contract negotiations as a trainee, expecting to come away with some sage wisdom, and when I entered the room, I saw the Contract Specialist setting up the conference table with a linen tablecloth, fine china, silver and then she served coffee and cookies when the DoD contractor arrived. Another Specialist, who always had a stogie hanging out one side of this mouth, brought a U.S. flag into the room and made everyone rise and pledge allegiance to the flag before getting started. Of course, the Specialists told me it was all tactics, to throw the hungry DoD contractors off guard. What I learned for sure, once I started negotiating on my own, was in the end, when the DoD contractor agreed to what I had deemed a fair and reasonable price, I knew I'd been screwed and there had been some sidebar negotiations going on between the contractor and the PM. It reminded me of buying a new car; I could never really pinpoint why I never felt that good when the salesman agreed to my offer, but the car salesman and his boss always seemed pretty pleased with themselves.

Being divorced I became closer friends with another trainee, Lana Lane, a good-looking, young divorcee who introduced me to the bar scene of the 80s. I wouldn't boogie on down long before I would meet my next husband. It was true that I had never had anyone throw a clay flower pot at my door because I wasn't at home precisely when I said I would be, but then he brought flowers and candy and profusely apologized that he'd just had a bad day. I might've shown a lot of potential at becoming what the Government called a professional, but "weenie" suited me better since I certainly lacked common sense when I married this bad boy. There was a lot more progressively bad behavior to follow.

Once again, I was going to need something else to get me through the next 25 years of another broken marriage and the real world. That would be humor; lots and lots of humor and there was plenty of it, even if some of it didn't seem particularly humorous at the time.

THE SOUTHERN COMFORTER.

J erry Jeremy was a suave, sweet-talking southerner with a thick, syrupy accent who had a real swagger and a fancy for the ladies. He achieved one of civil services highest pay grades before falling from grace and being asked to resign. That was another way the DoD sometimes tried to get rid of troublesome employees, but it rarely worked unless they really had the goods on them. I never got the straight skinny on what he actually did, but it must've been a humdinger or he wouldn't have resigned of his own free will. He didn't even go on to another Government job and get that glowing recommendation he'd been so good at passing out to the deadbeats. He did, however, go on to work for one of the largest DoD contractors that we did business with. That was something else I learned, that most retiring DoD civil servants, or military PMs, go on to second or third careers, usually with the DoD contractors they once worked with as civil servants/military. Heck, when my time came, so did I.

I discovered I was one of the few people in the building that could actually understand Jerry's thick accent when he spoke, since

I was a southern girl too. I found myself in the role of translator, along with my real job. Jerry, along with at least three other men I knew had all recently worked as civil servants in eastern Asia, each of whom married eastern Asian women, except for Jerry. Jerry had "sponsored" a few eastern Asian's travel to the U.S. but Jerry had just recently married for the first time to a woman who was a former military commissioned officer, also born in the Deep South. They met at one of the many mandatory Navy "all hands meetings." The workforce had another name for them. They called them "all feet meetings" since they were so clumsily done and always stank. There would be a lot of "all hands meetings" throughout my career. I truly believed Jerry wanted to be faithful to his new wife, and maybe he was. This was prior to cell phones, and it wasn't long before I became suspicious when I started taking mysterious phone messages for him from women other than his wife (a lot of them from the eastern Asian women he had sponsored). I also learned that while Jerry respected me and kept it strictly professional between us (at least for awhile) the grapevine still had me as a part of Jerry's "cabbage patch." The cabbage patch was comprised of various other women (most under the age of 40) who worked there, who, over time, Jerry would try to convince just exactly why he swaggered. It sometimes got pretty dicey for Jerry, since some of the cabbages would get jealous if Jerry didn't take them to lunch often enough to suit them, or sit next to them at happy hour at the Officer's Club. You see, lunches and happy hours were where all the shenanigans played themselves out "back in the good old days" before smoking and drinking became such bad things.

Happy Hour at the Officer's Club on base was a Friday night ritual. It was an old building too, with the musty smell of dried booze in the carpet that would stick to the soles of your shoes and a blanket of stale smoke that would envelope you as you walked in. If those walls could talk! Some of the regulars at the bar had been there since WW II ended! The bartenders had more dirt on the bar crowd than there was on the floor. Jerry and members of his cabbage patch could always be found there on Friday after work.

Who was there, who left with whom, who left alone and who left a few minutes after the one who left alone, was fodder for Monday morning gossip.

When my first marriage started to fail, Jerry was right there to comfort me. He encouraged me to go away to a month-long in-residence training course at an Army installation (which would include the Thanksgiving holiday). This particular Army base was a contracting school for the military as well as civilians. It was located in the middle of nowhere in desolate, gray, cold and depressing surroundings. Nevertheless, the in-residence mix of military and civilian students attending tried to make the best of it. Talk about partying like it was 1999! Still, I managed to graduate at the top of my class. And surprise, surprise, little did I know that Jerry had recently separated from his wife and planned to drive all the way from Florida north to his family's home a little farther north, for Thanksgiving. He somehow never mentioned it to me before I left for school. School was located close enough to make it practical for me to drive instead of flying since I'd be living on the base for four weeks with no rental car. Since my car had broken down the week before I left for school, I was fearful it might not even make it to school in the first place. I decided beforehand not to drive or fly home for the Thanksgiving holiday and had mentioned it at work. Jerry apparently then decided to take one small detour on his way north for Thanksgiving and arrived at my room in the Bachelor Officer's Quarters early on Thanksgiving Day, purportedly to see how I was doing in school and to see if he could make me a little less lonely on Thanksgiving. He invited me to go have Thanksgiving with him and his family, but I declined. He tried to change my mind, but for once my common sense prevailed. It never came up again.

It seemed Jerry just couldn't help himself. I recall one going-away party that I attended, along with the rest of the cabbage patch, where Jerry made his fashionably late entrance, only to start flirting with a potential new cabbage named Gina Gerard. Jerry had already thrown back a few, as had all the partygoers, including me, so the stage was set for anything. It was during the time of the 80's punk rock movement, and one of my fellow employees and partygoers had brought his collection of punk rock music. Even the most conservative civil servants were moshing to the beat. The problem was, Gina had a rather large, on again off again boyfriend nicknamed Moose and he was also there. The party came to an abrupt halt when Jerry and Moose "took it outside." I would forever have the indelible memory of Moose sitting on top of Jerry in the host's front yard. In exclamation of his prowess, I saw Moose literally slam down a bottle of Bailey's Irish Cream on the counter in the host's kitchen where most of it splattered onto the ceiling above, before he sucked down what was left into his already massive belly. Needless to say, work the next week was better than usual with Jerry offering up everything but the truth about how he got his shiner. And, in spite of Moose proclaiming to be gallantly protecting Gina's honor, Gina wound up being Jerry's main cabbage for quite some time after that. Seems Jerry was the gallant one after all. As the story went, it seems Moose's fist had made contact with Gina's face on one too many occasions and she finally left him for Jerry.

I lost touch with Jerry. He truly proved out the old adage that you're only as old as you feel. I heard he actually finally settled down for good when he remarried his first wife for the second time and they retired in where else, the Deep South.

ROACHES ARE CALLED PALMETTO BUGS IN FLORIDA.

There are many palmetto bushes in Florida and because the roaches that live in these palmetto bushes are so much bigger than regular roaches, that's how they got their name. If there was a WWII barracks building still standing in Florida 40 years later, you can be sure it would be infested with palmetto bugs they couldn't get rid of.

Thank goodness someone warned me to always turn my coffee cup upside down on my desk at the end of the day. The palmetto bugs came out at night and feasted on the remains of the day. That's another thing about Government folks. . .everyone is always eating at their desks because food is always abundant, and since the janitorial contractor never performed like they were supposed to, there was plenty of leftover food everywhere. Not to mention the "Roach Coach," a mobile food truck that came to the back door of each of the Navy base buildings early in the morning. Every morning you'd hear someone going up and down the hall shouting, "The Roach Coach is here!" Even with all the leftovers from the Roach Coach, one of the palmetto bugs favorite snacks was the leftover residue in the bottom of coffee cups. Those bugs would crawl into a coffee cup that was left upright and would gobble up whatever was left. They especially liked their coffee with cream and sugar, but black was OK too. I never got my coffee cup as clean as those bugs could; given the opportunity. Even forewarned I guess it was inevitable that I'd come in one morning and find a "floater" in my cup when I'd accidentally left a half cup of coffee at the end of the day. Thank goodness this was prior to the invention of the sticky tab, because these roaches also loved eating the glue off Government pre-printed address labels. You could hear many a new and unknowing DoD Contracting Clerk shout in complaint to anyone within earshot as she licked away at a label with no glue left that the Government address labels were obviously supplied by the low bidder since they were defective. If they only knew the real reason there was no glue left! Their alternative was using a test tube shaped plastic water dispenser with a red sponge tip on the end that was made specifically for that purpose. They'd remove the sponge end and fill the plastic tube with water and then squeeze the tube to get water on the address label. Those little tubes worked pretty well until the roaches discovered them and ate away all the little red sponges.

One early morning after the base exterminators had been there, I heard screaming from the back part of the office. I went back to see what the commotion was and found Moana Moore standing on top of her desk screaming while the retired Navy yeoman grabbed his broom and started sweeping roaches out the back door as fast as they came pouring out of the walls, floors and ceilings. His broom was always kept nearby for just such occasions and there were many occasions; each time the base exterminator came and went.

It wasn't unusual to hear screaming coming from different parts of the building at anytime during the day. It was like a car or house alarm today, no one even stopped what they were doing when they heard the shrieking. Someone was always opening a drawer, or a reference book, and having a bug crawl out. And seeing dead bug body parts everywhere, especially strewn up and down the hall and in the bathroom, was so normal, only new employees paid attention. After the incident with them pouring out of the walls, floors and ceilings, the only roaches that still made me pause briefly were the ones I found in the drinking fountain, and then only if they were still moving. I've lived in Florida for most of my life, and while I'd seen my share of roaches and palmetto bugs, I never experienced anything like that again.

IT'S GETTING HOT IN HERE. . .SO TAKE OFF ALL YOUR CLOTHES.

As if the nasty bathrooms, disgusting water fountains and palmetto bugs weren't bad enough, you always had summer weather to look forward to in a WWII barracks building. In Florida, winter is wonderful, but in the summer it gets real hot, and real humid, real early in the year and stays that way for a real long time. I loved Florida, but it's hot if you don't have air conditioning. It was always a challenge to try and figure out how to dress comfortably and professionally for a hot and humid summer Florida day in that old WWII building. I remember one guy who routinely took off his shirt around noon and worked in his white undershirt. As an Army tenant on the Navy base, the Navy base Commanding Officers' budget never seemed to have quite enough money left in the fiscal year to turn on the Army tenants' air conditioning, even though the ice cream shop across the street, the local cafeteria and the federal credit union didn't seem to have any problem getting their air conditioning turned on. But what I didn't realize at the time was that the real reason my building had no air conditioning was because of the age-old

Army/Navy rivalry, which continues to this day. Uncomfortable doesn't even begin to describe the picture of a building full of civil servants who rarely work anyway, coupled with the fact that it's over 90 degrees inside. I was lethargic most summer days. One particularly hot, sticky day I was so miserable I couldn't take it anymore. I'm one of those unfortunate people that perspire to the point where you can see the perspiration on the outside of their clothes, including the front and back of the crotch of your pants; I think you get the picture. Here I was, trying to be professional, walking around with a visibly wet crotch. Nice. I went to the top civilian manager in the building whose office was on Mahogany Row (all the managers had mahogany desks while the rest of us had standard issue metal military desks) and told him that if he didn't try a little harder to get the air conditioning turned on, I was going to be forced to go the Navy base Commanding Officer and wring out my panties on their desk. Miraculously, within three days there was air conditioning.

LET'S DO LUNCH!

L unch was revered. There were no time clocks to punch on the Navy base. The Government workers were on the honor system, and back then you only filled out and signed a time card at the end of two-weeks. Most civil servants took as long as they wanted for what was supposed to be a half-hour lunch, but still left for the day as if they'd only taken a half-hour lunch. You see, the Government doesn't officially pay their employees for their half-hour lunch, but in reality, they pay big. And, you won't get fired for taking a long lunch hour, unless your cheating became tantamount to gross fraud.

When BRAC closed the Navy base in the late 80's, I knew how fortunate I was to have a new place to go. It was a beautiful new building on state donated property next door to a state college. It would be the new home of the Army, Navy and Marines that supported the Contracting of training for the DoD. It was in a still relatively uninhabited part of the city and there were not many restaurants yet, and no malls nearby, like near the old Navy base. The building literally sprung up in the middle of the woods and it was a beautiful piece of architecture. It had taken years for the DoD contractor to complete, and was way behind in cost and schedule (another thing that runs rampant among DoD contracts) but it was worth the wait, if not the money. It was built to resemble a Navy ship and the land and landscaping were carved out to look like the rolling waves of the sea beneath the ship.

Unfortunately for some, with the new surroundings came a newly imposed requirement that each employee have a scannable photo ID badge. At the time, it wasn't really that big of a deal except for the employees who were grossly cheating on their half-hour lunch. These badges were scanned by a card reader which opened the automatic doors when we entered or left the building. At the time, 9/11 hadn't happened and they weren't capable of recording the time or the date, so the badges were just ever so slightly worrisome to the long lunch bunch.

That was, unless you had "Lurch" for your supervisor. He was nicknamed Lurch because he lurked. He lurked everywhere. You never knew where he was lurking. You see that tree moving? Oh, it's not a tree . . . it's Lurch. Lurch had a thing about cheating on your time card. He had to be the only supervisor I knew that actually did, because it was hot work in the summer sun. Not to mention he was one of the biggest offenders of cheating on his own time card. That's another thing you find a lot of, especially in Government; hypocrites. He used to tell his secretary to turn the lights on in his office as soon as she got there in the morning (7:30 a.m.) so everyone would think he was in too. Then, he'd come sashaying in around 9:00 a.m. and just tell anyone that had been looking for him he'd been in a meeting. Anyway, Lurch would hide in the parking lot, behind trees, bushes, cars, anything he could find, and lay in waiting for one of his employees to leave the building for lunch. Then he would follow them in his car to wherever they went and then all the way back to work. That was another thing I learned about most Government supervisors that didn't take long to figure out. They'll do anything to avoid doing real work, always opting instead for something they can handle, or get perverse pleasure in, like hiding behind bushes hoping to catch their employees taking a long lunch hour.

But, since Steve Stanley didn't work for Lurch, he still felt pretty safe and continued to tempt fate each day by taking his daily lunchtime jog on the Government's dime. By this time, the new and improved smart card had made the scene. Almost every office has them now and they can pretty much track where you are for most of the day, making it almost impossible to sneak out of the building for long, unexplained periods of time. Before that, Steve scheduled all his meetings for 10:00 a.m., every morning, or so the message he wrote on his white board permanently reflected. It was also much easier to disappear for long periods of time on the Navy base since all the program managers, engineering, and logistics folks we worked with were located in other tenant buildings and we almost always had meetings in someone else's building. With the new building I and my teammates were now a cozy little family, co-located on three floors. No one had to leave the building, unless they wanted to. Our old Navy base Contracting conference rooms were reserved for the meetings held between DoD contractors and Government Contract Specialists, so if you needed to have a meeting with a team member engineer, you had to take a stroll over to their old WWII barracks building.

So, Steve would stroll leisurely out the door of our new building every morning just before 10:00 a.m. It's funny that no one (no supervisors, anyway) ever seemed to notice that he always took his gym bag with him to all his meetings. Then one day I had an 11:30 a.m. doctor's appointment and my doctor's office just happened to be on the way by a beautiful city park located a short "jog" from our new building. That's when I spotted Steve at 10:45 a.m., jogging in the short-short, slinky little jogging shorts he favored. And, of course, I was just one more of many other employees that knew this was a daily occurrence. He didn't work for Lurch though, and he never got caught.

IS THAT A GUN IN YOUR POCKET, OR ARE
YOU JUST HAPPY TO SEE ME?

Gun nuts, you don't hear much about them until you unfortunately hear about them on TV. Unless, of course, your supervisor almost shoots himself and it makes the rounds of gossip. But then it's perfectly understandable why he'd be packing heat at the grocery store; you just never know when someone is going to put their hand on your banana. And, even though that wasn't the case on this very scary day in the history of the Chulevista neighborhood grocery store, you could never be too careful if you lived in that part of town. My boss, Stan McMurray got up one morning and put on his preferred weekend-wear of tight-fitting Wranglers, western belt, flannel shirt, jean jacket and cowboy boots. He was going shopping all right, but not for groceries. He was shopping for a girlfriend and someone had told him he should go to the Chulevista grocery store to meet women who liked real men. And, since he'd heard guns turned Chulevista women on, he packed his rod in case he got lucky. Unfortunately, this wasn't his lucky day. Stan had forgotten to put the safety on his 9mm that he had tucked in his inside jean jacket pocket. He accidentally reached inside his pocket pulled the trigger and BOOM! Thank goodness nothing was hurt, except Stans pride. Now, you'd think with all the fun we all had at Stan's expense when we found out, it should've pretty much cured him from carrying a gun, right? Well; not exactly.

Unfortunately, the Global War on Terror happened and with that came threat levels. Nothing revives a gun nut like a call to arms. So, when our resident Government lawman, Security Department Chief Randy Ruckster, put out an all-hands email asking for anyone who had experience with guns to come forward so he could deputize them and have them defend their country if need be. Well, you know Stan was Johnny on the spot. There was one small problem; Chief Randy didn't have the authority to deputize anyone. He didn't even carry a loaded gun himself. He was, after all, not paid much more than a Contracting Clerk. And he was the Chief of the Security guards, not the police. Only the threat of terrorism would eventually cause our then Commanding Officer to even think about giving Randy bullets for his gun. So, when Stan packed his car trunk (and person) the next morning with enough guns to either properly impress Chief Randy (or take out all the smokers in front of the building that were taking their ninth smoke break of the morning) he had nothing but good intentions. And, when he pulled his car up in front of the building, opened his trunk and his jacket and invited Randy to see what he had, that was the fastest anyone had ever seen a smoker move.

CLYDE, I HARDLY KNEW YOU!

For some reason that I never understood, civil servants are the only ones to ever make "Don't Ask, Don't Tell" work, long before we even knew what it meant. Civil servants never come out of the closet. Everyone knew who was gay; it was just never an issue. But then there was Clyde, and he presented a new set of problems. Clyde desperately wanted to be Clare and nothing was going to stop him. Not even the fact that huge fake breasts, pancake makeup, and mini skirts would ever disguise the fact that he still had a face that would stop a truck. Before he became Clare, he looked like a 50 year old Lynard Skynard groupie with stringy, greasy long hair. Not to mention the bald spot in the middle of the greasy long hair and a pair of very bad legs. Clare would also give new meaning to the next big DoD plan to fight the dwindling workforce by cross-training. Fouled up as this great plan also was, cross-training of Government civil servants in several career fields was in vogue and our crack Human Resources Office could be thanked. I didn't think the fact that Clare cross-trained in hair styling in her spare time, in addition to being a Government engineer, was actually what they had in mind. Nevertheless, as a hair stylist, Clare revealed all the many innovative ways there are to cover bald spots; always stopping short of a wig or hair transplant surgery (that just wouldn't be natural looking).

It took three all hands meetings and more cultural diversity training than any of us had had in our entire careers to set the stage for Clyde's metamorphous from male caterpillar into Clare's female butterfly. You see, imagine if you will, trying to tell a building full of Government right-wing, bible-thumping conservative Republicans that they could actually now be fired for something else besides gross time card or travel voucher fraud, if they dared speak ill of Clyde. . .um, Clare. Yes, there were trying times ahead. No one would know how trying until the transformation from Clyde to Clare was truly complete. Up until the time that Clyde actually had the transformation operation, his doctor (or so the Government managers briefed the workforce) required that he dress like a woman for a full year beforehand. It was all part of the transformation process to see if he was really serious about becoming a woman. That didn't really much bother most of us, since Clyde had been wearing one earring and eyeliner to work for years. But there was something that bothered the little old ladies on the third floor where Clyde worked. You see, there was the small matter of which bathroom he would use, since, so far, he'd just been dressing like a woman, but still using the men's bathroom.

Many a hastily called midnight Executive Steering Committee meeting (ESC) consisting of our top management executives would be held, now and in the future, to discuss this and all the other important issues these stellar Government executives had to deal with on a daily basis. The workforce would receive this and all other Grand Poohbah ESC guidance from our immediate supervisors who would love to call impromptu staff meetings to pass the word, not to mention waste some time.

THE CENTER FOR EXCELLENCE
TURNS INTO THE CENTER OF EXCREMENT.

I t was of little concern to all the highly paid Government research and developers that worked in the old WWII buildings and now in our beautiful new building, that they had never managed to get rid of the palmetto bugs on the Navy base. Nonetheless, we were a DoD agency involved in high tech research and development (R&D) and officially named ourselves and our new building, "The Center of Excellence." Next, they added a department that was solely responsible for awarding R&D grants to DoD contractors for various and sundry research projects. One such costly research grant was awarded to one of our local DoD contractor neighbors in the research park. This local contractor would be paid on a cost type contract until they figured out how to get rid of fire ants in Florida. To truly understand a Government cost type contract is to love one. The Government pays the contractor for their R&D efforts in solving a problem posed by the Government until the contractor came up with a solution, or the Government decided they didn't want them to continue (usually when the money ran out), no matter how long, or how much it cost. All the contractor had to do was submit monthly cost and progress reports together with their invoices for payment and have them approved by the Government. And, before they ran out of money, they had to ask in writing if the Government wanted them keep on working and if so, request more money. That is the nature of a cost type Government contract; the cost or length of time to complete the contract cannot be predicted accurately enough to make it a fixed price because the technology is unknown. Do you suppose there are a lot of cost type contracts awarded by the DoD? Do you think most DoD contractors ever found a solution to the Governments R&D problems? Precisely.

As everyone knows, fire ants *are* a big problem in Florida. Fire ant populations damage livestock and crops, not to mention the number of people being stung, which is especially important for the hundreds of thousands of people who are highly allergic to the ant's sting. After many years, and many dollars spent though, the funding well ran dry and the grant that had been awarded which involved the rearing and the release of fire ant decapitating flies had to be terminated for convenience. Yep, you heard it right; they created flies in the lab that bite the heads off fire ants. Actually, the larvae of these flies, which are parasitic on fire ants, eventually kill the ants in which they develop, and the flies harass other ants at the mound, reducing the ants foraging efficiency. According to the public news release announcing the award of this Government grant to the local Florida DoD contractor without competition, because only within the Center of Excellence community of Government R&D experts and DoD contractors did the know-how exist to rear enough fire ant decapitating flies for large-scale release. Not to mention, despite the time and money spent on this research grant, the productivity of the fire ants in my back yard (and my neighbor's back yards) remained unchanged.

Then, as if there wasn't enough for the ESC to mull over each week, my workplace went from being the Center of Excellence to the Center of Excrement overnight after the shit hit the wall one night in one of the bathrooms on the second floor. No, really, the shit literally hit the wall . . . and the floor and the ceiling. Someone had flung shit on the walls, floors, and ceilings for some poor unfortunate DoD janitor/contractor to discover, report and clean up. So began a chain of events that spelled yet another SNAFU. And to think, no one would've even known about it, if it hadn't been for the cameras Chief Randy (remember him, the Chief of Security) ordered installed *inside* all bathroom stalls. After another midnight meeting, the ESC had to come clean with the workforce, so to speak, about what had happened. But this was only after an employee spotted one of the not very well installed cameras above them, peering down at them inside a stall. That's when a complaint was filed with the Human Resources Office. Then, once it got out, you better believe, the shit really hit the fan among the angered employees. One would think that if they didn't have enough money in the budget to actually make the cameras outside of the building work, they might not have the money to actually install working cameras in all of the bathrooms, but that's where you really have to understand how a DoD executive mind works. Apparently, Randy got the approval to put the cameras in the bathrooms, but was too busy thinking about his soon-to-be glory days of catching the perpetrator on tape when the wise old wizards of the ESC told him to "Make sure the cameras are installed in the common area only, where everyone only washes their hands." This was the beginning of the end for Randy. There was so much made over the cameras, we were never even briefed on whether the perpetrator was ever apprehended. One good thing came out of it. They purchased working cameras for outside the building; the result of negotiations between management and the union after the bathroom camera fiasco.

DID I SAY THE EXECUTIVE *STEERING* COMMITTEE?

How about Executive *Stupidity* Committee? The group was composed of eight men and two women. The ESC tried desperately to emulate the board and CEO of a large corporation and its shareholders or the President and his cabinet, but it came off more like the Wizard of Id and his minions. Other attendees were allowed by strict invitation only. I was allowed into the inner sanctum of the ESC meetings on several occasions since I was a "staffer" in my last years in Government. Loosely translated, being a staffer meant I was some important person's highly paid gopher. There were lots of staffers who from time-to-time would be invited on a strictly "need-to-know" basis to attend some small part of the ESC meeting that would occur on a given day, so that they could go out and do the Wizard's business. A "need-to-know" basically meant you were the lucky minion that got to be the gopher for some lowly task the rest of them were way too important to actually do. ESC members acted like they put their pants and panties on differently from everyone else in the building. On one gopher task, as I sat in the back row of the auditorium like room, soaking up every last word from the Wizard, I mercifully drifted off into a daydream. I imagined each of the eight men, standing up, pulling out their "members" and proudly placing them on the lovely mahogany table they sat at each week, and then letting the two obviously token women decide who had the biggest member. If they did it that way, there wouldn't have to be any more inane ESCs to discuss whether Clyde should use the men's or ladies bathroom. In her daydream, whoever had the bigger "member" would always get to make the decisions, and if they were absent, it fell to the next member with the biggest member. If only.

PORNO MAN NUMBER 1, INTERNET CHILD PREDATORS, DATE RAPE AND SEXUAL HARASSERS.

Computers entered most DoD workers lives around 1982. I remembered when they brought those behemoth Zenith 248s into the building on the Navy base. They were greeted with trepidation by most of the workforce. The same retired Navy yeoman that had gladly swept roaches out the back door decided that there was no way he was going to use a damned computer. Shortly thereafter, he retired from his second career as a civil servant. Other Contract Specialists saw the advent of computers as an opportunity for DoD to now downgrade everyone into non-professional positions, now that we'd be doing our own typing (whether you knew how to type or not). As it turned out, it wasn't the computers or downgrading they had to worry about. It was something called the Standard Procurement System (SPS). The SPS was a commercially available software program that had supposedly proven itself out in the commercial market place, or so the Government's General Services Administration concluded when their Contracting Officer awarded the commercial contract to the low bidder for mandatory use of SPS by all of DoD Contracting personnel. It was required to have all the functionality required by the Government performance specification and was guaranteed to revolutionize and standardize the cumbersome DoD contracting process which used multitudes of existing and incompatible DoD legacy systems. After many, many delays and much money, the Government was later forced to admit in 2001 before Congress' Armed Forces Services Committee that SPS didn't actually have the DoD contracting required functionality it was touted to have. But that didn't stop SPS from being officially forced down DoD throats in 1994, already years behind in schedule and cost. It would only get worse. It quickly dawned on me that in addition to just plain typing, I was now doing a lot of data entry I'd never done before. If that wasn't bad enough, SPS couldn't handle the numbers of employees forced to use it and the computer would freeze up in the middle of a contract document. It would take hours, sometimes days to do something that should take a few minutes. The good news was no one was downgraded. They continued to pay the same high salaries to the professional Contract Specialists, now for typing and data entry too. Remember, now everyone who worked in the Contracting series also had to have 24 hours of business in a move to improve the education of the acquisition workforce. With the implementation of SPS the college educated acquisition workforce were now reduced to zombie like data entry clerks entering endless multiple data into an unresponsive computer system. To this day, there are mile high stacks of "workarounds" to try and get the SPS to do what they called "generate" a contractual document. That translates into lots of extra hours and taxpayer's dollars spent initially keying in and then re-keying the data multiple times in order to get the SPS to spit out a document that can be used. Stay tuned for more on that costly SNAFU later.

Others looked upon the arrival of the computer as a godsend. As the computers were replaced, each more state-of-the-art than the last, they had to create a special computer group that managed our Local Area Network (LAN), made sure our shared drive was backed up each night and made sure they fixed any problems we had with the computers and printers. I started seeing a lot of all-hands emails coming from the LAN folks, telling us that some of us were printing out too many lengthy documents, and it was causing a real problem with our network of printers and bogging down the whole LAN. They warned "That you knew who you were, so stop, or else." They continued with these threatening emails until one day, yes, that's right, another special ESC meeting had to be convened. It seems the problem didn't go away and the LAN folks had started officially searching for the print-crazy person.

The Government mentality is a real oxymoron. If management were presented with a problem, if they ever actually bothered to admit a problem existed, that would require they solve the problem. If they never admitted a problem existed, well, I think you get the point. I had tried for years to get one of my many supervisors to just admit to me, behind a closed door, that he knew that much of what I was tasked to do was a ridiculous waste of time and money, or just downright wrong, since the more money that was thrown at a project meant it was completely politically driven and no matter how hard I tried I could never get it delivered on time and within budget. I never got anyone to admit it.

The ESC had never seriously thought about what they would do to the person when they found the print crazy person, and when someone eventually brought it up, they put on their Wizard hats and decided they'd let the person's supervisor handle it, once they caught them. Now it turns out this person wasn't just printing out too many long Government documents, they were printing pornography, by the reams. Seems Peter Palmman (aka Porno Man) was a real *hard* worker, if you know what I mean. Turned out he'd sometimes work 12 hour days and never once asked for overtime or compensatory time. Again, since no one ever gets fired from civil service, the ESC was in a real stew about Porno Man. You see, Peter Palmman was the male supervisor to an all female group and his direct supervisor was also a woman. Ultimately, the ESC did exactly as they'd decided earlier; they left it up to his female supervisor to decide what to do with him. Shortly thereafter, Peter was demoted from his supervisory position and made a staffer, like me. It didn't take the rumor mill long to out him. One Monday morning I would be summoned by my supervisor to attend an unscheduled staff meeting, to announce we had a happy new addition to our little staffer family. Guess who? The majority of Government employees start as early as the Government's flexible time keeping system will allow which is 6:00 a.m. That means they can leave as early as 3:30 p.m. and Katy bar the door at 3:30 p.m. I wasn't a morning person and chose to work 8:30 a.m. to 5:00 p.m. There wasn't one evening that went by as I passed Porno Man's cube as I was leaving for the day that he wasn't still working at his computer, just as hard as ever.

Now the next guy, Ralph Roamer, turned out to be an internet predator of underage girls. I thought he was just another strange dude; there were certainly more than enough of those to go around, you couldn't give it too much thought. One day, he just wasn't there anymore. He actually got fired. Turns out he worked for a DoD contractor who was under contract to the DoD to provide his services, but he wasn't a civil servant. He had a government-furnished cubicle right around the corner from mine. He was a newlywed who drove an expensive sports car, and could usually be seen out at lunch, with at least one other younger woman other than his wife, most of the time two or more squeezed into a booth with him in the middle, like a sandwich. I knew something was up with Ralph, call it female intuition. I had once been assigned to work with him on a team project. When one of my sexy dressing young co-workers was also assigned to the team, I could see Ralph's eyes undressing her. He didn't even get an all-hands meeting or an impromptu staff meeting after he was arrested. I found out by reading it in the newspaper.

Then there was the local date rapist and sexual harasser, Barry Boneman. I had heard for years that he was a date-rapist, from two women who were known to be reliable sources. I shared a cubicle with him at one time. He used to put raunchy paperback books inside the Government regulations and read during work. He was from an ethnicity that always got him extra points on his resume.

One day, a woman filed formal sexual harassment charges against him and Bonemans' supervisor was forced to address the problem because sexual harassment was now against the law and he had no choice. The investigation went on forever it seemed and the supervisor ultimately had a nervous breakdown. Boneman, however, never wavered. They eventually transferred him to an entirely different building and an entirely different career field where he wouldn't be a supervisor anymore and that was the end of that. He maintained his salary, and would eventually get a buyout, just like me. After he retired he went to South America and married a young woman in her early 20s. His accuser eventually took a job elsewhere because she was made to feel like a leper.

POMPOUS PILOTS ASLEEP AT THE CONTROLS.

Another thing you learn over time about Government supervisors. They are all pompous bullshit artists that do nothing. I didn't have one supervisor that didn't love to talk about themselves, as long as it had nothing to do with work. Lester Lyerman was different though. He made things up about himself. I always figured he had low self-esteem and somehow felt the need to prove to everyone how smart and talented *he thought* he was. He never once admitted that he'd basically fabricated his entire life, but as he told more and more people, and these people told other people, one day he pissed off the wrong person who had suspected it was all lies and they decided to expose him. Not that it made any difference other than to give everyone a good laugh. He claimed to have been Jesuit-schooled. He was a Methodist. He claimed to have a law degree. He had been a law-clerk when he was 20. He said he was a concert pianist. He played the organ at his church and for some lucky dinner guests. He told everyone he was a marriage counselor. He would listen and give advice to married friends at church who bitched about their marriages. He was studying to become an architect. He had a subscription to Architectural Digest. We called Lester "The Great Pretender."

Another thing about Government, especially supervisors, they are so cheap they squeak when they walk. How many people do you know that actually purchased a Flo-Be and gave themselves a haircut? Or use one of those little rubber change purses you have to squeeze at the top and bottom to open? Or consistently post things for sale on the electronic bulletin board like broken TVs and shabby Christmas decorations? Or drink the cheapest beer made even though they can afford the best? Or refuse to ever hire a babysitter, even when they make a lot of money? Or still wear leisure suits because they're too cheap to buy new clothes? Or still drive a first year make Toyota Celica that used to be red and now was pink from sitting in the sun all day? Or, when they're eligible to retire, don't? I actually had a supervisor tell me that the only reason he didn't retire was where else could he get a job doing absolutely nothing and make so much money doing it?

BARNEY AND HIS BAND OF FIFES.

Not only did terrorism unfortunately bring out all the Government civilian gun nuts, it turned our staff of civilian security guards into gun toting morons. Don't get me wrong, they were morons before, now they were morons with guns. You see, this was the opportunity of a lifetime they'd all been waiting for. They always had guns, but no bullets. They were never given the authority to shoot them, lucky for all of us. They were however, able to turn what was our beautiful, high tech looking, three story professional building located on beautifully landscaped grounds, into a tacky-quasi "military compound" if you will, complete with a barricaded entrance to the parking lot, armed by the Band of Fifes. You can't just requisition a boatload of barricades and have them delivered and put up overnight. So, to begin with, they made a barricaded entrance with those orange traffic cones you see everywhere. It looked like one of those test courses you see on TV. Yeah, those will sure keep the terrorists out; or confuse them anyway. Then, when the requisitioned barricades did arrive, probably a year later, if you don't think the place looked tacky before, you should've seen it then. Now there were giant white and red *plastic* barricades which replaced the orange traffic cones at both the front main and rear entrances to the parking lot, not to mention a make-shift "security shack" which was erected at the main entrance. Even the ESC had to do their part and give up one of their many privileges to fight terrorism. You see, the rear entrance to our building was simply the entrance to a parking lot for the privileged few. We only had so many Fifes, and not enough to man the rear entrance as well, so they just barricaded that completely with the tacky looking giant white and red plastic barricades where no vehicles could enter. They were still plastic. The real mystery was that while the main entrance and rear entrance were barricaded, the rest of the perimeter consisted of acres of property surrounding the building that only had a small hedge enclosing it. Do you think they thought about barricading the rest of the perimeter? Much like any other real problem, when our ESC got together in one of their midnight meetings, and they planned to make our lovely high tech building safe from terrorism, they simply overlooked the rest of the open perimeter. Or, maybe it just fell into the "too hard" category, as most things in Government do. Or, maybe it was a SNAFU. Eventually, they actually requisitioned giant concrete flower pots to replace the red and white plastic barricades. They sat on one side of the parking lot for months until one of the weird facility guys (think Charlie Manson) got around to getting out the only forklift there was and started moving the flower pots into their proper defensive positions. They were flower pots; but getting flowers or plants in them, that was years later. And years and years later they still hadn't found Osama Bin Laden but they finally put up a chain link fence around the entire perimeter of the property.

Now, you don't think perhaps all this new power led to perhaps a few incidents whereby the security guards may have overstepped their boundaries just a little? Of course it did. They now had the authority to search each and every vehicle that entered the parking lot and believe me, until it finally dawned on them that this was way more work than they'd ever had to do before, they had a blast doing it. There were a total of about 1,200 civilian and military employees that worked there. Management finally figured out how much productivity was being wasted because we each had to plan an extra hour to get to our desk in the morning in order to have time to have the car searched first. Talk about a traffic jam. At least it turned out to be a pleasant experience for Clare (aka Clyde), who was thrilled when they searched her car because in doing so they unearthed her favorite shade of Estee Lauder coral lipstick that she'd been missing. She was so appreciative she posted an email to our electronic bulletin board to praise the security staff.

Lest we forget that once you got inside the door you might be subjected to a bodily search. I suspected the bodily searches is what pushed Randy, Chief of the Fifes over the edge.

PORNO MAN NUMBER 2.

Chief Randy Rauster was randier than most knew. I had a personal experience with a bodily search that seemed to go awry. One day as I entered the building I was wearing a gray pants suit, with a perfectly tailored blue silk shirt underneath, black boots and a black purse. I'd noticed in the past, even before the searches began, that Randy had never quite been able to look into my eyes when we talked. This particular morning, his eyes lit up and he said "Well, good morning, you're looking mighty sharp today, could I get you to open up that lovely suit jacket and let me see what's inside?" He didn't ask to search my purse. I never took off my jacket at work but being the dutiful civil servant that I was, and in an effort to do my part to make the building safer, I hesitantly opened up both sides of my jacket. Randy looked long and hard; supposedly to make sure I wasn't carrying any weapons. No, he didn't touch me; but if a look could be felt. I couldn't stop feeling like I'd been violated in some small way until it got to the point that it bothered me so much I told my supervisor. As mentioned, you don't want to bring a real problem that requires actual action to the attention of a Government supervisor. And, as many a tattle-tale knows, the tables wound up getting turned on me. I was accused of grossly exaggerating the incident, until *I* felt like *I* had done something wrong. I dropped the whole thing.

It wasn't much later, though when I felt vindicated. Peggy Plumpton, the local tight ass Chief of Information Security, shared an office with Randy. She was looking for a file in Randy's desk drawer when she happened to discover Randy's stash of porn. It all seemed just a little too coincidental to me. There was only a short period of time that had passed after our Commanding Officer had been forced to call that special "All Hands" meeting to brief the entire civilian workforce on the Center of Excrement episode (including you will recall, the cameras being placed *inside* the stalls). Randy would be escorted out of our building by one of his own Fifes. They put him on administrative leave pending possible termination. I was shocked to hear they had actually mentioned possible termination. Remember, there aren't many things than can get Government employee fired, even downloading porn using a Government computer which simply got Porno Man Number 1 a demotion and transfer to my department. I heard later that poor Randy had a mild heart attack while on administrative leave. His doctor said it was caused from the stress of being falsely accused and threatened with termination. So, Randy didn't get fired. They got rid of him the only way they could. They gave him a full medical disability retirement which resulted in Randy getting a larger pension than he ever would've gotten if he had made it to full retirement eligibility.

THE $400 HAMMER AMONG OTHER THINGS.

We contract weenies were at the end of the contracting cycle (in more ways than one) and while we were all stewards of the taxpayer's dollars, we were the last in the line at making sure the Government was going to pay "a fair and reasonable price" for training as we awarded all those large dollar value Government contracts to one of the many DoD defense contractors. We were like Rodney Dangerfield, we never got any respect. By the time the PMs approached us with the requirement from the Army, Navy or Marines, they had already wasted so much time that whoever we were buying the training for was completely pissed off. So, what that meant is the Contracting folks always had to make up for all the wasted time up to that point. Then the PMs just wanted us to hurry the hell up and award a damned contract to someone so they could get their cash bonus.

After the contract was awarded it was then administered together with our sister Contract Administration weenies to make sure the Government actually got what they paid for. The Government inspection and acceptance process may be worse than the contracting process, if that's possible. We contract weenies got a really bad rap with that $400 hammer that was actually negotiated and purchased by our sister administration weenies as a spare part for a flight simulator we'd procured. You see, administration weenies were responsible for negotiating a fair and reasonable price for all the spare parts that were necessary to keep the flight simulator up and running, after it was delivered. We contracts weenies sent the administrative weenies a list of those spare parts that our spare parts weenies said the simulator would need to support it, and the administrative weenies negotiated the price to be paid and awarded a contract to buy the spare parts. That $400 hammer was a spare part that needed to be replaced in some toolbox. Not only was it a specialized hammer, but it's perfectly legal for a DoD contractor to mark-up a specialized hammer with overhead, general and administrative expense and profit, but of course, those little details always seem to get left out of the story. These DoD contractors are also supposedly audited by another arm of Government, another check and balance, and the Contract Specialists and Contract Administrators are required to consult these auditors and ask them for a recommendation on all the individual cost elements of the contractor's cost proposal before we make an award. So why did only the contract weenies get stung? Because they needed a scapegoat, like they always do, and our group were easy targets.

Later, still trying to show how totally inefficient the Government was (hey, you won't get any argument from me on that), Al Gore would appear on David Letterman and the Government would be a laughing stock for having procured an ashtray using a design rather than a performance specification, thereby making it the most expensive ashtray ever purchased and obviously a big waste of the taxpayer's money. He was right and the Government went through some major changes while they got rid of a lot of Government design specifications and replaced them with performance specifications instead. But, when you really get down to it, I saw that wasting the taxpayer's dollars is really how everyone in the Government kept their jobs. And despite this particular Vice President's noble efforts to streamline the Government, guess what? It's worse today than ever, far worse. The bureaucracy is bigger than ever, no one can really change it; no one. As long as there are politicians, there will be lobbyists and there will be bureaucracy. Some have tried and tried and failed and failed. Some are still trying. Two recent contracting horror stories come to mind; Frank Rich's New York Times article "Suicide Is Not Painless" about Charles D. Riechers, 47, the second-highest-ranking contracting officer in the U.S. Air Force, who killed himself by running his car's engine in his suburban Virginia garage. Mr. Riechers' suicide occurred just two week's after his appearance in a front-page expose in The Washington Post. The Post reported that the Air Force had asked a defense contractor, Commonwealth Research Institute (CRI), to give him a job with no known duties while he waited for official clearance for his new Pentagon assignment. Mr. Riechers, a decorated Air Force officer earlier in his career, told The Post: "I really didn't do anything for C.R.I. I got a paycheck from them." The question, of course, was whether the contractor might expect favors in return once he arrived at the Pentagon. Mr. Rich's article also reminds us that Mr. Riechers' Pentagon job, managing a $30 billion Air Force contracting budget had been previously held by a civilian named Darleen Druyun, who in 2004 was sentenced to nine months in prison for securing jobs for herself, her daughter and her son-in-law at Boeing while favoring the company with billions of dollars of contracts. Ms. Druyun's Pentagon post remained vacant until Mr. Riechers was appointed. He was brought in to clean up the corruption! When I attended a mandatory Government contracting course in Washington, DC in 1996, Ms. Druyun was the luncheon guest speaker. I sat at the same table with her and her male military aide. Talk about a guy that looked scared. I didn't like anything about Darleen and mused she was way too full of herself. Sometimes I had good intuition, not that it ever really did anything except get me in trouble.

Then, of course we can't forget Watergate, Whitewater, Halliburton, Blackwater, etc. The list goes on and on; some are specifically contracting corruption, some just Government corruption. I read an Associated Press (AP) article that the Army had spent $2.6 billion on hundreds of European-designed helicopters for homeland security and disaster relief that turn out to have a crucial flaw: They aren't safe to fly on hot days, according to an internal report obtained by the AP. Makes my withdrawn DoD Hotline complaint (don't believe it if they tell you there will be no reprisal) pale in comparison.

DANCES WITH WOLVES AND OTHER GREAT INDIAN NAMES.

All of my friends had a good sense of humor; it was a prerequisite. So, shortly after "Dances with Wolves" came out, we got together and came up with our own version of Kevin's Costner's Indian names. My supervisor at the time, a highly intelligent but lazy bi-polar, male chauvinist pig would be Fat Ass Sitting, since he did that so well. He would sign anything anyone put in front of him. It was a well known fact that none of the supervisors want to be bothered. They don't want to read what is written, but when they did, they'd pick something of little importance to question, like punctuation, or grammar. Heaven forbid one of them ever actually read anything for substance. So, anytime I would get frustrated because someone was harping on something of no real importance, and taking up a lot of time, I'd just say "Gnats and Camels." If asked to explain, I would. Most times I was ignored. Government supervisors will gag and choke on a pesky little gnat all day long but when it comes to the real content, the real meat; that camel with a hump would go down so easily it's as if they'd took a tablespoon of mineral oil first. Fat Ass

Sitting was a champion at both. But when it came to hiring new employees, now there's where he took a real personal interest, new *female* employees, in particular. He especially liked the portion of the process that involved reviewing their resume; but of course the somewhat more personal part of the resume that listed the professional organizations they belonged to outside of work, which sometimes included their hobbies. He was single and in perpetual search of Miss Right, even if he was Mr. Wrong. If he could get an "in" with a new lady by knowing in advance what professional organizations they belonged to or what their hobbies were, he could feign a similar interest, or even go so far as to join that organization. As if. He was morbidly obese, rude, and crude. I lived in fear when he sat directly across the conference room table from me at meetings. The buttons on his shirt near his belly were extremely challenged to stay put; I feared one of them would pop off at any moment and projectile itself across the table and into my eye. He would also rail on an on that he just couldn't date women his own age because they all seemed to have masculine features. When I heard that for the first time, I roared with laughter. One good thing about working for the Government is that you can pretty much tell your boss off and they can't fire you. They can transfer you, they can make you miserable, but they can't fire you. I asked him if he'd taken a real, good, hard look in the mirror lately. He didn't even flinch. He thought he was the perfect male specimen. He would go around telling everyone all about the potential new female employee's personal life. The new employee would be doomed before they ever set foot in the door because Fat Ass Sitting was a big gossip. All the top managers were. Forget ethics. What a shock to the former pro-football cheerleader and professional dancer who was now a Contract Specialist that Fat Ass Sitting hired sight unseen. She had been judged, ridiculed and labeled as an "air-head" before she ever spent her first day at work. Fat Ass Sitting, of course, could barely contain himself waiting for that first day. She turned out to be beautiful, smart, had a great body and of course, was young. He had high hopes. His hopes were dashed as quickly as you can say Fat Ass Sitting. Did I mention she was also a great judge of character?

My Indian name was Screeches Like Owl. Enough said.

Then there was Shit for Brains. Now, this guy was one of the smartest men I had ever known, but for the most part he'd taken the easy way out his entire life, given a choice between how many hours he'd have to devote to doing it the hard way. His lament was always that he got kicked out of the group where he worked with me for a while. Of course, he'd usually also always fess up that it might've had something to do with the fact that he and his cube-mate Dominick talked sports all day, which happened to back up to the cubicle of the future supervisor of the branch we all worked in together.

Next we had Sits on Fences. Talk about procrastinators. I knew he'd never actually made a decision in his life; the decision process was bypassed and eventually always just became overtaken by events. However, Sits on Fences got credit for saving the Center of Excellence by awarding one of the largest DoD contracts ever awarded (at the time) and back when the Center's head was on yet another BRAC chopping block list. When our Commanding Officer submitted the report to the BRAC Committee in Washington that this huge Army contract (scheduled to be awarded soon by our Navy Contracting department) would possibly not get awarded because of the Center being on the BRAC list, the Army went to bat for the Navy by sending their biggest guns to Washington to lobby for the Navy and convince the BRAC folks that Sits on Fences contract must be awarded and the Center could not close. It's the only time I ever knew of the Army supporting the Navy, or vice versa. Of course, all the jobs in that building, a lot of which were Army civilian employees and military too, were also in jeopardy if BRAC shut down the building. So, Sits on Fences saved the day by having been assigned this huge contract to get awarded. Unfortunately, the camaraderie between the Army/Navy only lasted as long as it took to get the Center off the BRAC list.

There was Pounds Keys Hard. This guy had real anger management issues. I had never heard anyone pound a computer keyboard quite like this guy. I also recall one night at a party seeing him kick the chair over that his wife was sitting in because she dare say they had to leave early because Pounds Keys Hard had an early tee time.

Bear Climbs Mountain had climbed many a mountain, only to fall, get back up and keep climbing.

IT'S WHO YOU KNOW AND WHO YOU BLOW.

Yes, the Governments' management glass ceiling is still relatively shatter proof; for the most part. You still won't find the same numbers of women in management, although the numbers are increasing. Most of the women I knew would shatter the glass ceiling legitimately, but let's just say the ones I vividly remember, sadly, the stupid ones, all have glass in their knees. Lacey Lourdes had to have surgery on one of her knees. Not to remove glass, but after a drunken weekend water skiing accident at a party attended by Mike Manfred. Mike swam out to a drunken Lacey's rescue, swept her up in his arms and carried her safely to shore. I didn't know his name at the time. Later, someone would tell me when he came into the cafeteria that that was Mike Manfred, and what an asshole he was. I commented on how he didn't look like an asshole, and I knew a lot of assholes. He liked Lacey . . . a lot. Of course, a lot of guys liked Lacey . . . a lot. Shit for Brains told me on more than occasion that he really liked the perfume Lacey wore, it was sexy. Always one for seeking out new perfumes, especially those worn by sluts, I found out that it was called "Knowing." Yes indeed, Lacey knew. Lacey had the only successful "open marriage" I had ever heard of. Well, it was successful to the point that they stayed married for many years anyway. Her husband, Gary, was notorious for a bumper sticker on his very large SUV that read "I snatch kisses and vice versa." At least most of the women he propositioned couldn't pretend to be shocked. Even though I had always thought Lacey was dumb, I gave her credit for getting more out of her trysts than Gary every did. Lacey continued to get promoted beyond her level of competence until she finally "made" top management. One of the last flings I knew about was before I retired and was with Tim Thompson. He was married and notorious for all his extra-marital affairs. It seemed natural that Tim and Lacey would hook up. Whether it had anything to do with Tim, I didn't know, but Lacey started acting very weird at work to the point even management had to notice. Now, far be it from me to criticize anyone who's depressed from seeking medical attention, but Lacey seemed to be the poster-child for why not to take medication. Either her doctor couldn't get her medication cocktail just right, or maybe it was the combination of booze and pills. It started with silly little things, like spreading cream cheese on the inside of her arm, instead of on her morning bagel. She started teetering precariously atop the stilettos she favored. She dozed off. She slurred her words. Lacey and I would have a big falling out a couple years before I retired because I was assigned to a task that involved having to work with Lacey. I knew I wouldn't get much help from Lacey, but I tried. After many unreturned phone calls and emails, Lacey accidentally answered her phone one day. I exploded and wound up the conversation with telling her I always thought she was as dumb as a bag of hair, and well, you might imagine that it went downhill from there. She never spoke to me again, until long after I retired.

After I retired a friend from the 70's died of unusual circumstances. After his death, I learned that he and Lacey had become the best of friends. I attended a memorial happy hour for him at one of his favorite watering holes and Lacey was there. I buried the hatchet, but noticed things didn't seem to have changed too much with Lacey. She was talking, but obviously had already had a few, and was primarily looking in the direction of some young, handsome guy I didn't know and who was making the rounds from table to table speaking to everyone. Later, I heard he was the nephew of the friend that had died. Apparently, Lacey didn't know him either, but I knew it wouldn't be long before she did. Lacey couldn't concentrate and had now completely stopped looking at me. She quickly ended the conversation but not before insisting that we get together for lunch soon because she had some information about our mutual friend's death. I was intrigued and ultimately agreed. It turns out the entire purpose for the lunch was to make sure I knew they had been inseparable ever since my friend had gone to work for her and she was devastated by his death. After four or five vodka tonics, Lacey also told me their friend talked about me most recently and how disappointed he had been when he learned I was working as a contracts consultant for Kyle Reno. Seems my friend and Lacey shared a real dislike for Kyle Reno. Turns out they were actually both right about Kyle.

Then there was Gidgette Griffin. She was married to a retired military man, who true to form, was working on his second career for one the local major DoD contractors we did business with. She ultimately made her way through most of the guys who were interested in having sex with her, and eventually moved to another Government job in another state with a whole new group of men. She began the first affair that I recalled, with a skinny, nerdy guy. He was a real neat freak, and a great interior decorator. He was not gay. His very young wife had cheated on him several times in the first year of their marriage and then asked for a divorce. It upset him greatly and understandably so. He took up a new hobby, he started working out. Turns out Gidgette worked out too, right next to him, and the affair got a kick-start because he was a good listener. He became so smitten with her that they even timed it so they both arrived precisely at the same time in the morning so they could park their cars side-by-side and walk in and have breakfast in the cafeteria each morning (on the Government clock, of course). He tried so many different times to get her to leave her husband and marry him that she finally told him she was really leaving her husband, and to prove it she rented an apartment for herself. She paid for the entire seven month lease in advance, but never left her husband and never moved into the apartment. She finally broke it off with this poor guy and not only stayed with her husband, but moved on to her next affair. He would never trust women again. He wound up like Gidgette in a way. He'd dated so many of the people he worked with, he had to move to another state. I referred to Gidgette's next boy toy as "Mandingo," like in the book. He was a young, good looking, hunk a hunk of burning love with a fabulous physique that worked upstairs. It didn't take long for the word to spread and like the guys I worked with who waited for Christa to make her mail run everyday, all the ladies made it their business to know what time Mandingo visited Gidgette each day; you know, like that Coke commercial where all the ladies gather at the window to watch the construction guy outside take off his shirt and drink his coke. Next there was Chuck Ramie, who we soon nicknamed Chuck Layme. I saw him at one of the annual military Birthday Balls years ago. Yes, that's right, that's what they call it. Then there was Deandra Davis. She was so stupid she still thought the guy that promoted her was also going to marry her, even when he retired and moved into a retirement community with his wife of over 45 years. I loved to "catch them" riding down the elevator together at the end of a work day. Obviously, as soon as I got on the elevator, the air was so thick you could cut it with a knife. I always stifled a "Hey Deandra, how's tricks?" which was always on the tip of my tongue.

THE WORLD'S SMALLEST MARINE
AND BORN AGAIN CHRISTIAN.

I had the misfortune to have the world's smallest Marine as my PM on one of my contracts. The first problem, right out of the starting gate was that I was 5'8" and Buck Bruit was not an inch over 5'2", so he was already pissed off about that. You see, the Napoleon complex exists, and until you've worked with a small man, you don't really understand it. I would encounter many more small men in my career, and I had experienced the Napoleon complex. Add to the mix that Buck looked like the troll under the bridge and you get the picture. Buck was the head of the Government team which had to travel to our DoD contractor's facility for a progress review, which meant I always got to spend some real quality time with Buck and the rest of the team. His Napoleon complex was never more apparent than when he was chairing meetings between the Government and the contractor. If Buck didn't "lose it" at least once an hour by screaming and yelling very unprofessionally at the contractor about something they were doing wrong (which he usually turned out to be wrong about and later had to apologize for) then it wasn't a normal meeting for our Government team or the poor contractor.

Now I'm not saying that I don't have my own little neuroses, doesn't everyone? I was claustrophobic. Among other things, I didn't like riding in elevators. On one trip in particular, there were eight Government types, including me, all staying at the same cheap motel. One late afternoon after a stellar scream fest performance by Buck at the contractor's facility, the weary team of eight got into two rental cars and returned to the motel. Everyone's rooms were located on the same floor of the motel. Buck always insisted on that when the team travelled together. I have never understood people and elevators. It's like if they don't push and shove their way on to one that's already full, it's like there's never going to be another elevator. Being claustrophobic, I tried to make it a habit to never enter a full elevator. Unfortunately, this particular day I entered the elevator first, only to watch in horror as the rest of the team piled in. It was also a very small elevator, it was an old motel and a couple of my teammates were extremely overweight. The obvious then occurred; the elevator stalled and there I was, stuck in the back. Buck was in the front right corner. At first I tried humor and said "So, whose brilliant idea was it to see how many people we could fit in this phone booth of an elevator?" I couldn't breathe; panic started to engulf me. I felt like I might actually die of suffocation on this elevator, with these people, and I lost it. "Jesus Christ, get me off this thing!" By the time the elevator started to move again, Buck was seething, but I had no idea why or that it had anything to do with me. You see, in working with Buck, I had somehow missed that he was a born again Christian. Describing me as heathen might be a tad strong, but religious I was not. The next day, back at the contractor's facility, I noticed that Buck was more pissed off than usual, and it seemed directed at me this time. One of my teammates took me aside during one of the breaks and told me that Buck was very unhappy about my taking the Lord's name in vain in the elevator. Buck had mentioned that he might file a complaint with my supervisor when the trip was over. "Listen; if Buck does complain about you, I just want you to know something that might help you. Buck made me stop the car on the way to lunch today to go to the 7-11." I said, "Yeah, so what?" He continued, hesitatingly. . ."Well, he wanted to stop while you weren't in the car so he could get a Penthouse magazine." He then burst into laughter. I would go on to work with many more self-proclaimed born again Christians. Just think Jim Baker and Jimmy Swaggart. I heard later that when Buck retired, he became a prison guard. Super. Poor prisoners.

SMOKERS. . .GET THEE TO THE GREAT OUTDOORS!

I always thought Government smokers all had a look of desperation in their eyes. They didn't even know what hit them. First, it was just portions of the cafeteria that were designated as Non-Smoking. Then, they started having these things called "Great American Smoke Outs" where management would try to entice people to quit smoking for one day by giving them a free hot dog. Yes, a hot dog. Second, they completely banned smoking in the building. The smokers were now relegated to only certain tables on the outside patio to smoke. Or worse, they'd let them stand in a certain area near entrances/exits to the building. Finally, they banned them from certain exits and entrances. Now, which generation do you think the majority of the people that smoked that I worked with belonged to? Yes, the baby-boomer generation. Being of that generation, and knowing what we all know today, do you think a lot of them might be addicted to nicotine? Do you think the majority of workers that smoked when smoking was banned in the building were baby boomers nearing retirement age? You're three for three. But what you probably haven't thought about (or perhaps you have) is the amount of money wasted in the Government by retirement eligible baby boomers that are addicted to nicotine. Next, factor in all the pissed-off non-smoking Government workers who did very little work anyway, add their resentment at the numbers of smoke breaks the smokers took during the course of a day, week, month, year end and year out. I saw a lot of civil*ian* unrest. Some of the smokers only took breaks once an hour. Most never came inside except to go to the bathroom and eat lunch. If I ever needed to find Bob Kirkpatrick, I knew where to find him; he'd be smoking with Lacey Lourdes on the back patio. I could look out my window and see them smoking, flirting and yucking it up. Since Bob was a smoker, at least I knew where Bob was, I could never find the rest of the people that were non-smokers when I needed them.

KAYDE, THE CAFETERIA "LADY."

I admired the hell out of Kayde; no body messed with Kayde, she was one tough broad who had a vocabulary of curse words that would make any of the sailors blush. Mostly she stood behind the cash register in the cafeteria and made change. In her free time she partied at a local redneck bar. You didn't want to get to her cash register with anything larger than a $10 bill, unless you were spending at least $5.00. If they only could've trained the Government supervisor to motivate their employees like Kayde motivated us to have the correct or small change, I figured out they could've saved the taxpayer's billions. As if she was in need of an exorcism, Kayde's voice would begin to rise, her tone would deepen, her nostrils would flare, and her eyes would flash. It might've had something to do with the fact that Kayde was always hung-over. And if you've ever heard the term "road hard and put away wet" . . . well, that pretty much sums it up. The only thing that could cheer her up was a handsome dude with a killer body. Especially those that played along with her and let her come up behind them and grope them while they poured their coffee. That would make her roar with laughter. You could relax and serve yourself a little extra salad from the salad bar when we heard Kayde roaring with glee. That was the only time Kayde wouldn't bitch you out for trying to heap as much salad as you possibly could in the little plastic salad container they provided. She absolutely loved it when someone in the building invited her to an after work party. She was always the first to show up and the last to leave. That was, until one fateful party where she wound up flipping her old, beat-up car in a ditch on the way home to her double-wide mobile home located in the little neighboring town of Bathsheba. Kayde was never the same after that and believe me, neither were we.

GOVERNMENT GIRLS GONE WILD.

I was always amazed at the young girls that weren't necessarily even trying to get promoted who seemed to spend an inordinate amount of the work day wasting time by pursuing men, married and otherwise. And the men would spend a lot of their work days seeking out and gladly receiving these lusty ladies' attention. Then, the flirtations usually played themselves out at the local promotion, retirement, or going-away party, always held at some place called "Honkers," or "Headlights" it seems. These parties were the highlights (next to lunch) of most of the workers' days since they led such boring and pathetic lives. At one party, I recall Kitty Kumming was in rare form, as was the esteemed, brand spanking new young lawyer and the director of operations; Kittys' soon to be latest conquests. I pondered if Kitty was trying for a ménage a trois. Kitty looked how I always quite simply described as exotic. She was young and beautiful with large dark eyes, dark skin, dark, thick, long wild curls; even her tongue was dark. The guys could barely control themselves when they were around her; I speculated it must be the tongue. She also had a smokin' hot body and loved to flaunt it. The fateful night that ruined both the director of operations' credibility, as well as our new lawyer's marriage and reputation was the night Kitty brought Sisqo's "Thong Song" to life at "Honkers." When Kitty first made her appearance at the party, no one noticed she was wearing a gold thong that was peaking out the back of the top of her pants, but Kitty soon remedied that. She went to the juke box, dropped a quarter in the slot, and when "Thong Song" started playing, Kitty started gyrating . . . first towards the new lawyer and then the director of operations (who was nicknamed "Eyes Wide Open" since he'd just had a brow lift). From the crowd's perspective, it could only be described as lap dancing. It was truly the highlight of that promotion party until Pam Pukar drank herself into a stupor and ended the festive mood of the party when she threw up her false teeth in the bushes outside the front door (the bar windows were glass so those inside could see everything). The false teeth apparently met up with a rock in the bushes because the next day she called in sick. Pam didn't make it back until she got a brand new set of teeth.

BUT I'M REALLY SICK THIS TIME BOSS!

Then there was Cauldwell Conners, who came highly recommended by his current employer. You remember how that works, right? I tended to form my opinion of someone quickly, and Cauldwell was no exception. He seemed to tip toe down the hall. He was wishy-washy, pot-bellied, and young but not that young. A guy who was already doing the comb over of the few hairs he had left. He was the only small man I ever met who *didn't* have a Napoleon complex. He seemed shy and unassuming. He should've been nominated for an acting award for his many outstanding performances. He finally transferred and took another job elsewhere. I like to think I was instrumental in his demise, since I never let up in my bitching to Fat Ass Sitting to get rid of Cauldwell because I was sick and tired of doing all his work. Fat Ass Sitting had put him in the cubicle sitting next to a guy we called Big Bird, because he looked just like Big Bird, but he had the personality and booming voice of the Jolly Green Giant. My cubicle was immediately next to theirs, and I got to listen to all the great interaction between the two day in and day out. It was hysterical. I remember on one occasion Big Bird, who didn't make as much money as Cauldwell, asked him what "step" he was (there 10 steps in each professional GS series that equate to more dollars the higher step you are). Cauldwell told him he was a Step 10, which is the highest step you can reach. Big Bird was quiet for a brief moment and then he slammed his giant fist down on his desk, laughed and bellowed "And deservedly so my good man, and deservedly so!!" From that day on, Big Bird tortured Cauldwell relentlessly. Cauldwell started calling in sick a lot, so much so that his work had to be transferred to me and others in order to get Cauldwell's PMs off Fat Ass Sitting's back. That was when Fat Ass Sitting decided he had to take some sort of action that at least looked like he was documenting Cauldwell's poor performance. But since Fat Ass Sitting was also known to call in sick quite often, the documentation of Cauldwell's non-performance would fall into my lap on the days Fat Ass Sitting was out.

I was, of course, secretly glad to do it, and even took it upon myself to "counsel" Cauldwell about his poor performance. I was never one to mince words. I took Cauldwell into a conference room, just the two of us with no witnesses, closed the door and told him that if he didn't knock it off and either get himself straightened out or get a job somewhere else, I was going to put a potato sack over his head and beat him to a bloody pulp with a baseball bat. He was obviously under enormous pressure, apparently at home too. You see, in addition to his work woes, Cauldwell had a boyfriend that beat him up. Cauldwell would come to work with a black eye and an occasional limp. And, as if things couldn't be any worse, Cauldwell was addicted to cocaine. One Sunday night my phone rang at home and it was Cauldwell. He wanted to borrow $10 for gas so he could get to work on Monday. Not being the sympathetic type, especially where Cauldwell was concerned, I said absolutely not, and hung up. On Monday morning, I overheard Mike Mitchell telling Nelly Nelson that Cauldwell had called him on the weekend and asked to borrow $25. Then Nelly told Mike that Cauldwell had called her too and asked to borrow a hundred. Well, before the day was over, it turned out that Cauldwell had called pretty much everyone in the Contracting Department and had succeeded in borrowing a lot of money that would never be paid back. A couple days later, I ran around the corner to answer Cauldwell's always ringing office phone and it was from Bob's Rentals where Cauldwell had rented his TV. Seemed he was way behind in his rental payments and they wanted to know if I knew where they could reach him. Turns out, Cauldwell had actually sold the leased TV for cocaine money. It was not much of a surprise to anyone that only a week or so later Cauldwell announced he'd taken a new job in Chicago after Fat Ass Sitting gave him an outstanding recommendation. I was so thrilled he was leaving I arranged a going-away party for him, but I didn't invite Cauldwell. All the people he'd borrowed money from showed up and everyone had quite a laugh at Cauldwell's expense. I heard later that Cauldwell was eventually promoted again. Just like Big Bird might bellow, I was sure it was deservedly so.

CAT NAPS.

What is it about the term sleeping on the job that rings so true? Especially in the Government, cat naps are not just limited to the worker-bees, but top management. Listen, I'll be the first to admit how much I loved a nap, but never on Government time.

Maynard Hargrave was the head attorney (no pun intended), but sadly that didn't keep him from sleeping on the job at the most inopportune times. I recall one early morning staff meeting, where Maynard's head literally hit the conference room table when he fell asleep while an Army General was speaking. Do you think any of the very high ranked military (or civilian) attendees said anything? That's what's really scary. No one said a word. Maynard had quite a nasty bump on his head the next day too. I knew people that slept during church, but that was not terribly uncommon. And, as if to attempt to cover it up, he'd start every meeting by telling everyone he was a workaholic and he never slept. He said that's why you'd see emails from him at 3:00 a.m.

Maybe he had narcolepsy, although you'd think someone would tell us, or you'd think he'd get treated for it, wouldn't you?

Then there was Charlie Crimotti. I had already experienced Charlie's sleep deprivation at many a meeting that I had attended with him. But when he fell asleep during a presentation I gave during a conference attended by hundreds of DoD contractors and then woke up right at the end to ask a bunch of questions I'd already covered, well that was the last straw. I wasn't the only one to see him snoozing during all of the prior presentations thus far, so when he started asking his questions, I boldly said, "Hey Charlie, why don't you just go back to sleep?" For that I got my first and only round of applause in my life.

Jake Tommias just slept all day and that was that. There wasn't anytime you could walk into his cubicle and catch him awake. His best friend Lex, did all his work for him. Jake finally took early retirement on, what else, a medical disability.

And last but certainly not least, we can't forget the dumb as a bag of hair turned top Government manager, Lacey Lourdes, who I hear is still sleeping most of her workdays away.

WASTED DAYS AND WASTED NIGHTS.

Most Government meetings, especially staff meetings, and Government travel, are another surefire way to waste money, minute by painful minute, day in and day out, month in and month out, year in and year out. You see, Government meetings/travel are proclaimed to be necessary to make sure whatever it is you've been tasked to do is done with the proper planning and of course that it get's done. Let's just say that in reality, Government meetings/travel is a great way for the worker to actually avoid ever really having to do any real work. You can always hear someone saying they just don't have time to actually finish the project they were assigned, because they're always so busy in meetings or on travel. Then there is the difference between the meetings held at your workplace and those held while on travel somewhere else. I could count all the meetings I ever attended at work that had any sort of prepared agenda on one hand. So, since most meetings held at the workplace have no agendas, and no one ever really chairs the meetings, you can generally count on the person(s) attending the meeting with the biggest ego to dominate the meeting and therefore waste the most time. Now, that's not the way it's supposed to be. The Government teams are handpicked by their supervisors to insure an adequate mix of all the necessary personality types. The Government is big on Meyers-Briggs. They were called Integrated Product Teams (IPTs). So, the IPT leader is supposed to be a smart, take charge, agenda driven personality, who knows how to steer the meeting and make sure it stays on track. I don't know if King Kong was agenda driven or not, but his personality pretty much describes any team leader I'd ever had. The rest of the team was definitely composed of a mix of personality types. There was always one person who did all the work, one person who did nothing at all, and one person who always made sure we got off track no matter how hard the IPT leader tried to get us back on track. Believe me, this was the one teammate that always succeeded.

Now Government travel is slightly different, except for the composition of the team. You usually travel to a DoD contractor's facility, or the military installation that has funded your project/contract, for a meeting to discuss the progress being made, or more often not being made. There's always an agenda, but the Government doesn't prepare it. The Government always pays the DoD contractor to prepare it. Then, the IPT leader reviews it, makes changes to it and approves it before the meeting. It just wouldn't look good if the contractor delivered an agenda that the IPT leader had no comments to. That might look like we relied too heavily on the contractor to do the Government's work. Government travel rarely lasts less than two days, whether it needs to or not and it almost always involves either a Monday or a Friday and preferably both so you can combine work with an extended stay on the weekend on the taxpayer's dollar (your round trip airfare is paid for by the Government, you only pay for your lodging, etc. on the days you aren't working). Most civil servants love Government travel. Especially travel for the purpose of attending Government training that hopefully lasts at least five working days and can be combined with a weekend (again at Government expense). Government training equals party time. There are no tests given at the end of most Government training. They aren't called boondoggles for no reason.

This huge waste of time went for the all hands meetings too. Once or twice a year, whether there was anything to discuss or not, they gathered us all together to give us their version of the "The State of the Union" speech. The rest of the times were those disclosures of something that would make us uncomfortable and there were a lot of those. It was truly pathetic. The Government never honestly tells the workforce anything they need or want to know. Don't forget, the really important people, the Commanding Officer and the ESC, they put their pants and panties on differently from the rest, so they were the only ones who really knew the truth. After the fall of Enron, and hearing about how Ken Lay strongly encouraged all Enron employees to invest all their retirement money into only Enron stock, at the very moment he was selling his as fast as he could, was like deja vu. I would recall many a meeting where the workforce would be told one thing, and then, low and behold, a month later they'd find out just the opposite had happened.

IGNORANCE IS BLISS.

Now, I'm not insinuating that everyone in Government is ignorant. However, it certainly appeared to me there were an awful lot of really blissful ignorant people that I worked with. It also seemed that on those rare occasions when I did work with someone I admired, they usually turned out to be smart, but tortured souls. Most of the people were more like Candy Appleton; clueless. Fat Ass Sitting had assigned me to train Candy. That basically meant that until Fat Ass Sitting decided she was trained, Candy would be my shadow. Poor Candy. I was assigned a very important project and Candy was supposed to cut her teeth on this project with me. I had a meeting scheduled with Charlie Cipronetti, the second man in charge of the Army group I worked with on the project; he was only one down in the pecking order from an Army General for God's sake. He was an intelligent, good looking, well-mannered, well-dressed, well-spoken Italian who liked to smoke big cigars (that was back in the day of when smoking in the building was still allowed.) I desperately tried to convince Fat Ass Sitting that it wouldn't be a good idea for Candy to attend the meeting with Cipronetti since the chances of Candy blurting out something inappropriate or doing something stupid were almost a given. He, of course, disagreed and said it would be an excellent training opportunity. The next morning, Candy came bounding into my cubicle, like a big ole' Golden Retriever. I didn't get a complete look at her from head to toe from the other side of my desk. From what I could see, she had on what would be described almost as a Catholic school girl's jumper with a white blouse. She looked extremely conservative and I felt better. I tried to convey to her how important this meeting was, and how important Mr. Cipronetti was, and that Candy should not utter a single word during the meeting. She was just there to soak it all up like a sponge. Candy bobbed her head up and down, enthusiastically agreeing with me. I would not get a complete look at Candy's work attire until we started walking together towards the conference room where the meeting with Mr. Cipronetti would be held. When I saw her shoes, I yanked her by the arm and tried to pull her into another conference room along the way, but it was too late. Mr. Cipronetti was behind us. He was speechless, but as he looked Candy up and down from the top of her head to the bottom of her red fuck me pumps and little white lace socks, the cigar fell out his mouth. Then, he gave *me* a look that would kill. Candy didn't stay with the Government much longer after that. Thank goodness she was still in Career Conditional status or she'd probably be in some top management position by now.

LEPER, OR JUST A DEMOCRAT?

I never realized until well along in my Government career that most Government workers are Republicans. I am a registered Independent and would vote for any political party candidate if I thought they were the right person for the job. I think of myself as a former Democrat from the south that had morphed into a somewhat right sided Republican. I wasn't a bible-thumping, pro-Defense spending, pro-life, pro-war, homophobic left side of a Republican, although I was from the Deep South. I was more like poor ole Al Gore, a liberal leper, sans a bleeding heart. I didn't know if there really just weren't many Democrats/Independents in Government, or if they were all just too scared to say so. I'm pretty sure it must be the latter; because once the word slipped out that I voted for Al Gore, it seemed there were three times as many Republicans than I ever imagined. I would become the recipient of many unwanted emails bashing Democrats, from irate Republicans I didn't even know.

DAMIEN AND OTHER LEGAL EVILS.

The IPT oftentimes includes another member, the Government lawyer. They don't attend all meetings or travel, just those where their legal advice is requested or required. Now, the first thing you need to understand is that a Government lawyer doesn't make as much money as a private practice lawyer. That should clue you in. When I started working at the Navy base, I met my first Government lawyer; he was completely atypical from all the rest I would endure. My supervisor had directed me to get his help on writing a contract clause. I got to the word "fiduciary" in the clause and Bill Bummer paused. Being young and inexperienced, I thought I had cleverly anticipated what the lawyer's question was going to be. I then blathered on with the definition of "fiduciary," without ever being asked to do so. Bill Bummer looked at me like my second grade teacher had the day I got my hand slapped with the ruler. He glared when he said, " I KNOW what fiduciary means."

And then there was Damien Dexter, the other end of the spectrum of Government lawyers. Damien was the lawyer who did nothing, ever. He could only be described by all those who knew him as completely useless. I would often show up for a scheduled meeting with him, only to find the door closed . . . and locked. I'd knock, there would be no answer and I would start to walk away and then I'd hear noise from behind the door. After a few extremely awkward minutes, but quite an amusing few minutes for the lawyer's secretary and me, the door would open and a disheveled Damien would appear.

I would unfortunately receive a request for more money from one of the DoD contractor's I worked with, insisting that one of my Government IPT members had required the DoD contractor to provide something that was outside the scope of the contract and they should be compensated. This would be a very lengthy chapter in my career, and one of the most distasteful. One of the worst parts of the whole ordeal was the fact that Damien was assigned to be the Government lawyer on the claim. This meant I would have to travel with Damien and other members of the IPT in order to vet the claim. Their first stop was Arizona for depositions with the contractor's lawyer. Damien routinely wore a jogging suit, sneakers and a baseball cap to the Government only meetings. No one gave his work attire much thought until I glanced over and noticed shortly before lunch one day (not after) that Damien had his feet stretched out on top of the conference table and was supposedly reading through the contractor's claim. The brim of his cap was pulled down covering his eyes. All of a sudden, I heard snoring. It was Damien. Now, Damien wasn't just another Government sleeping beauty, he was much, much more.

I had never been deposed before and had no idea that it was the Government lawyer's job to prepare me for the deposition that would be conducted by the DoD contractor's lawyer. It was immediately evident, however, that the Government side of the deposition was not going well and Damien didn't know what he was doing (and neither did I). Since this unfortunate business would go on for years, there would be many more lawyers; some Government, some DoD contractor's lawyers, but I learned how important it is for the Government lawyer to know the law.

Next, we had to travel to California to the contractor's facility for discovery. Damien was flying separately and agreed to meet us separately at the contractor's facility on Monday morning at 8:00 a.m. When we arrived, Damien was no where to be found. He had not contacted us since we parted with him on Friday evening on our way to the airport in Arizona. The contractor would not let us enter the building without our lawyer, as per previous agreement. This was in the days prior to cell phones, so I asked to use the contractor's phone where I immediately called the hotel where we were all staying to see if he checked in. He hadn't. It never occurred to me that I should've called him on Sunday evening to confirm. I considered that would be insulting. I called the hotel where we had all been staying in Arizona and found he had checked out on Friday. I called Damien's office to find out if they had any information on his whereabouts. They didn't. Somewhere around noon, the contractor felt sorry for me and the Government engineer, and let us in so we could start our discovery by reviewing all the documents we had requested be provided, without the Government lawyer present. Damien called my room on Monday evening, as if nothing had happened, wondering where we were all going to dinner. Damien simply claimed we were all mistaken, including the contractor; the meeting was not supposed to be until Tuesday. When I returned to work, I wrote a scathing email to Damien's supervisor, the lead attorney, a smart woman named Annastia Abercrombie who we jokingly referred to as the Caribbean Queen because of her accent. Annastia was smart, but was still a supervisor. If a problem were brought to her about one of her lawyers, you basically knew in advance that nothing would ever happen. After receiving the email, she actually came to my cubicle, sat down in my guest chair, pulled it close to my desk and in a barely audible whisper asked me what it was that I actually wanted her to do about Damien? I was so shocked that this powerful woman had come to my cubicle, but was stunned at the question. I flashed on appearing before the Commanding

Officer to explain *my* insubordination. I said, "Nothing, I just had to get it off my chest." So, it was never mentioned again and nothing was ever done to Damien. I, however, became a pariah to most of the rest of the legal staff. Not much later, though, I happened to run into another one of Damien's fellow lawyers in the hallway and he was smiling and laughing. He'd apparently heard about Damien's escapade and my email and he stopped me. We shared quite a laugh, which made me feel better than anything else had so far. Damien went on to another Government job at another military installation shortly thereafter. When he requested several years later to come back to his old job, Annastia actually told him no.

WHO MOVED MY CHEESE?

Yes, the best-selling book about Sniff and Scurry, Hem and Haw, mice facing big change in their lives and learning how to accept it. My supervisor passed one book around to all five staffers, with a signature slip attached to it. Each one of us had to read it, sign that we'd read it, and pass the book on. The fact that they would pass a book around for us to read scared me, I wasn't quite sure why yet. Shortly after reading it, I got summoned to the office of the second Navy civilian in charge at the time, a member of the Senior Executive Service and he quizzed me on the book. He was a small Italian man named Paul Palantino and he had graduated from a prestigious college in Alabama and spoke with a southern drawl. He pressed me to tell him which mouse I most associated with, Sniff or Scurry. I felt pretty silly. Paul was a big baseball fan and worshipped Yogi Beara's sayings. One of his favorites was "When you come to a fork in the road . . . take it." It wasn't long after meeting with Mr. Palantino and I was told I was the command representative for what I was told was the prestigious People's Focus Group in Washington, DC. Now I was just plain scared.

GOVERNMENT BRANDING AND ERP, PARDON ME!

So, they moved my cheese, and sent me off to the People Focus Group to learn about branding. The Navy activity that I worked for decided they needed a brand name, like Coke, or Nabisco. I'd never heard of such a thing in Government, but this was a new era and I was told to get on board before the train left the station. The Navy had, of course, hired a DoD support service contractor, to conduct the series of branding meetings. All I remember is that it was another one of the most painful experiences I'd been through, sitting in group gropes and circle jerks with fellow Government employees for hours on end, putting together collages from it seemed like thousands of little pictures clipped from magazines and newspapers trying to come up with something that gave us a real identity. Then, I'd have to attend endless lunches and dinners kissing up to people I didn't know, and didn't want to know. The resulting brand shall remain as nameless as it was senseless. They were making up words, like touchpoint. There was no definition for touchpoint that I could find in the dictionary in 2002 including the one they made up; "A touchpoint is any product, service, experience, or transaction that gives a constituent an impression (functional and emotional) of your brand. They are how you match expectations to experience for your customers." Excuse me? If you look up touchpoint in the dictionary today, it does now exist and it simply states "the point of contact, esp. when products or services come into contact with a customer." That's why I hated words like that and the people that make them up. Why not just define it as point of contact, which is clear and concise? If I had a dollar for every focus group I'd worked on I'd be a very rich woman. Focus groups cost a lot of money, are a gigantic waste of time and are always chaired by some beltway bandit. So, I took the fork in the road and decided I didn't want to be there and I didn't want to be a member of the People Focus Group. So, at each meeting, I started questioning everything the bandits came up with. I didn't have to go to many more branding meetings after that. I wasn't a team player.

I knew that wasn't the end of it, there would be reprisal. It came in the form of ERP, Enterprise Resource Planning. Don't know where they came up with those words either (like touchpoint), but as a staffer, I was going to be responsible for training the workforce in how to use it, even though at the time I didn't even know what it did. I soon discovered it was just another messed up computer software program that we all had to learn to use. The workforce immediately tagged it, "ERP, Pardon Me!" like they had burped up some extremely distasteful cafeteria food after lunch. All I knew for sure was that ERP was why we'd all had to read "Who Moved My Cheese" and what I had to really be scared of, but didn't know it until then. If I was going to train it, someone had to teach it to me first and so I was therefore assigned to the ERP implementation team. The guy they put in charge of the ERP implementation team was a stressed-out guy from Kentucky and former Vietnam Vet who tended to tighten his jaws, grit his teeth, and not like women very much, especially me. His name was Elmer Egost and he had been getting cluster headaches every since Vietnam. I tried to steer clear of Elmer and that was the way Elmer liked it. I got a crash course in ERP and was then thrown to the wolves of the workforce. All the employees that I subsequently trained were suspicious, cynical and hated ERP, and I couldn't blame them. They only trained me (as well as all the other trainers) enough to spit out a pat little spiel. To this day ERP doesn't work properly, and the workforce still hates it. SPS revisited.

KYLE RENO.

I met him when he was one of those young whippersnappers I mentioned before; he was a part of the entitled generation. He was cocky and thought he knew more than he did, and cared more about himself and his social life than his job. It was all about me, me, and me with them. They wanted rewards and never criticism. There are more of them than ever today. I saw these children and young adults in action. They simply do not take no for an answer and they think they are perfect just the way they are. This goes far beyond the "spoiling" of my generation. I had one young woman in her second year of college that was hired for a temporary summer job only, but if she did a good job she was told it could very well turn into a permanent entry position. Melody Millennia was counseled more in the short time she was with us than most people are throughout their entire career. Now, I know what you're saying. You're saying this whole book is about deadbeat Government employees, so why single her out? Let's just say the deadbeat Government types at least knew and adhered to the unspoken rules of the official workplace, waited until they had their three years tenure to start blatantly taking long lunch hours, etc. After being counseled, Melody continued to wear midriff baring tops which revealed her pierced naval, was never at her desk, was late to work, took long lunch hours, left early most days, called in sick a lot and talked back to you when she was being mentored. I told her that even though there was no formal dress code, if she really wanted to impress the older, more conservative higher ups, she just couldn't dress like that at work. It fell on deaf ears. She was devastated when she was not hired for a permanent job after the summer was over.

I will say Melody was the extreme example. Kyle wasn't like that, except for having extremely high self-esteem, and thinking he knew more than he really did. High self-esteem had worked well for him and no one seemed to care about his pulling the answer out of his ass when asked a question. No one checked his answer. They should have. He started working for Fat Ass Sitting, in my branch, in the mid 90s. He wasn't even 30, he was single, good-looking and I was, well, older, and had just gone through my second divorce. His first day, my friend thought he would make a good match for me (she was married to a younger man) so she invited him to join our lunch bunch that day. I had just divorced a bad boy, and my tingly spider senses told me to beware. I heard Kyle was somewhat on the lam from Arkansas, partially because he fathered a child and split trying to avoid child support. Not that Kyle was interested in an older woman anyway (and who could blame him). Older Government women are not like Hollywood cougars. He had fresher, firmer fish to fry. He was a math major and was soon wowing top management by volunteering to teach regression analysis. He got the nickname of BYF (Brilliant Young Fanatic). By this time, I had moved out of the branch and on to my Contracting Analyst job, and Kyle would come visit me, supposedly just to say hello, but he'd always manage to ask me and have me answer one tough contracting question before he left. I caught on, as did many of the older, experienced women he routinely visited, but that was OK. I worked in the Policy Office now, and one Monday morning, Darryl Draggers, our resident fancier of the art form known as topless dancing, strolled into my cubicle and sat down. Darryl rented out two rooms in his house to topless dancers. He started telling me a story about his recent weekend visit to the Sex Toy Megastore. At first, I just glared at him, but then, it started to get interesting. He told me that while he was browsing the shelves, he had just happened to glance over and see Kyle Reno with Patty Piccata. Now, Patty Piccata was married to Peter Piccata, Kyle's new best friend. Darryl said they pretended not to see him and quickly exited the store.

It wasn't long after that and Patty would join my exercise class during lunch and started to really lose weight. She was a pretty, young girl, and had just had her first baby. Peter was a control freak and was another with a Napoleon complex. Soon, Patty left Peter. Then the rumors started circulating that Patty had been seeing Kyle long before she left Peter. They both denied it for a very, long time. They were still denying it by the time Patty and Kyle moved in together and Peter and Patty's divorce was final. Peter and Kyle still continued to be friends.

Shortly thereafter, I got a promotion to the Program Management career field, and thereby escaped the Contracting Department forever. I moved to the second floor. Kyle quickly got a promotion from GS 12 to GS 13. I knew Kyle didn't have the knowledge or experience for this job, as did many of the other employees who had also applied for the promotion that had been there a lot longer, and had a lot more experience and practical know-how than Kyle. I heard Peter was still one of Kyle's biggest fans; OK, let's just make it clear, all Government workers are ass kissers, but Peter wins the award for ass kisser of the year to Kyle, who'd broken up his marriage. I just couldn't understand it. Kyle eventually dumped Patty for another pretty young thing, and then another, and another. He got another promotion too. I rarely saw him, or heard much else about him, except that he took care of his loyal followers/admirers. He hadn't started punishing those that weren't loyal followers, yet, he hadn't made it to the top rung of the ladder. . . yet. It wasn't long before I heard that several of the now much younger than Kyle females were promoted beyond their capabilities. One had the face of an angel and the voice of a baby and was promoted to work directly for him. It was the perfect bad cop/good cop relationship. You were certain when listening to Angel Baby that she was the sweetest, nicest girl in the world; even when she was telling you to go screw yourself. My now deceased friend had once attended a party where Angel Baby was in the pool with Kyle, in her birthday suit.

Just like so many before me, I would go to work for a DoD contractor after I retired, as a contracts consultant. I finished my first consulting job and would go on to work as a contracts consultant for the Government off and on for the next few years.

Kyle went on to get promoted again, and he promoted Angel Baby beneath him, so to speak. Angel Baby had moved so quickly into a highly graded position that she was able to afford to buy a house on the site of the old Navy base, that exclusive, expensive perhaps toxic Disney-like development I mentioned earlier. I heard Kyle had finally reached the top and was a power to be reckoned with and that he was an asshole. Reminds me of the punch line of a joke about all the body parts trying to decide who was boss: "They all decided that the rectum should be the boss because even though the others do all the work... the asshole is usually in charge." Kyle had succeeded in reaching the rank of the most important civilian in Contracting. By now he had a couple of broken engagements under his belt and many more girlfriends. I thought he'd probably remain a permanent bachelor. Oh, and remember that lack of camaraderie between the Navy and the Army? Kyle would make that soar to new heights. The Navy had always gotten credit for all the contracting dollars ever awarded to DoD contracting contracts whether they were Navy or Army dollars and the largest percentage of contracts awarded were always Army. It was just the nature of the long standing arrangement and the source of much of the rivalry between the two. Kyle would single-handedly spearhead the effort (by getting the ear and gaining the confidence of the most important Army civilian in charge) to win the Army their total independence from the Navy contract weenies and start getting credit where credit was due for each and every dollar obligated by the Army. No one held that against him; it was the way he went about it. I had met this most important Army civilian briefly, and heard how smart he was. The fact that he allowed Kyle to get so powerful, and potentially dangerous to the good name of the Army activity he represented, always baffled me. But, it's all about money in the end, isn't it? Kyle was obligating more and more Army dollars and putting them on the map. And remember Peter? Peter was kissing Kyle's ass more than ever in the hopes of getting one of the three recently advertised promotions to GS 14 that Kyle had available. Peter was either stupid, scared, extremely forgiving, or diabolical (keep your enemies close, etc.).

Kyle was a political animal but I did not know that he had actually started exacting his revenge against what he considered disloyal employees. I did not grasp what that truly meant until I got a call from Konstance Kisyuraz, Angel Baby and Kyle's gopher. Kyle offered *me* a job as a contracting analyst consultant to support them in setting up their own Army contracting/contracts policy department, now they had officially won their independence from the Navy and no longer had to follow Navy policy. I would work closely with Konstance. I was excited to be doing contracting/contracts research, this time for the Army, and I loved the work. Konstance admittedly didn't know much about contracting, since it wasn't her primary field, but it didn't keep her from being unreasonable with everyone (including people with much more experience and knowledge than her) about contracting facts she simply did not know, but made up as she went along. She was also a bitch. She was a big girl, tall, with large fake breasts, a large backside, and a big nose that was so far up Kyle's butt it was more disgusting than usual, even if ass kissing isn't that big of a deal in the Government. Sometimes it can just go too far and it had. She also had a funny walk which accentuated the size of her rear end. I probably wouldn't have noticed her walk except one day I followed the three Musketeers (Kyle, Angel, and Konstance) back into the building after lunch and that's when I really saw her walk any distance. The three of them were always together. I heard people say they actually got nervous when the three of them came into the cafeteria together (which happened on a regular basis). Konstance would do or say anything Kyle told her to do or say. So would Angel Baby. I soon understood that was his plan all along, to get as many mouthpieces as he could; the fact that they were females was even better. He had his male mouthpieces too, one that had been following Angel Baby around like a dog for years and it finally paid off for him. Part of her deal was that she got to bring Tim Bean with her when she became Kyle's right-hand woman. Tim was as bald as a cue ball, short, chubby, had a lisp and was just, well, unattractive. He didn't impress me with his lack of knowledge either. Angel Baby and Tim looked like Beauty and the Beast.

Anyway, Konstance had recently transferred over from the administration department and worked directly for Angel Baby who worked directly for Kyle. One of the things I had always told Konstance was that I never wanted anything to do with the SPS. I had heard it was a software nightmare from my fellow co-workers. One day, in a meeting with Konstance and Angel Baby, it was announced that there was an SPS crisis and there was a critical task that had to be completed immediately and they did not have enough people or expertise on hand to do it. Kyle had proclaimed this SPS task was the biggest priority his contract specialists had until it was completed. I asked why they didn't simply hire a DoD SPS expert to come in and do the job, like they always did, especially since it was at the end of the Government's fiscal year and the contract specialists would be concentrating on obligating their expiring end of the fiscal year funding. Konstance scoffed at me and said that was impossible; there were only two SPS experts that she knew of, and one of them was already working for her, a retired contracting/contracts type turned DoD contractor, that attended the same meetings I attended and did similar work. The only other expert that she knew was already working part-time for the Navy, so there was no way they'd even consider her (since they were still warring with the Navy over their independence).

Konstance said her expert, Harley Harrigan, a good ole country boy, was already so overloaded that it was an impossible task for him to add to his already full plate. I discovered that Harley may have been a retired contracting/contracts type but he didn't know his ass from a hole in the ground. And he certainly was no SPS expert. He had such a full plate because he made mountains out of molehills with everything he was assigned to do. He kissed Konstance's butt; it was a real daisy chain. Also, with SPS, it's just not that difficult to learn, so no matter how much I might not know, I learned enough to know how little Harley knew. No matter how smart you supposedly become in SPS, until you know all of the mile high stack of workarounds that are required to actually get a contracting document released (and the workarounds change with every new release of software), it will always be overly time consuming and wasteful. I'm not sure anyone knew all the workarounds. I came to believe there was no such thing (or can there ever be) as an SPS expert.

Well, what happened next surprised everyone, especially me. I had continued to say during numerous meetings when the subject of SPS came up that that was the one thing I would have nothing to do with. All of a sudden, I found myself actually asking what would be involved in someone learning how to use the SPS. Again, Konstance and Harley scoffed and taunted me with my own words "I thought you said you never wanted anything to do with SPS? Do you want to do it?" I admitted I had said that, but there seemed to be a crisis at hand, and if they would be willing to teach me SPS, I'd be willing to learn it and try to complete the job for them. Besides, I liked the money.

They took me up on my offer, and it wasn't long before I learned personally how powerful Kyle Reno had become. As mentioned, he had gotten close to the main man in charge of the Army, Dr. Clarke. Dr. Clark was with the Senior Executive Service. Dr. Clarke was a distinguished looking man in excellent physical condition because he liked to work out. So did Kyle. Or, rather, Kyle started liking to work out once he found out Dr. Clarke was a fitness fanatic and frequented the local area gym. I just so happened to also work out at the same gym as Dr. Clarke and would oftentimes find Kyle and Dr. Clarke in deep discussion by the barbells. Dr. Clarke didn't like the fact that the Navy employees working for the Army were allowed to work under a flexible work schedule that allowed them to work 9 hour days and take every other Friday off, called their Regular Day Off (RDO). Dr. Clarke mandated that unless you were on paid vacation or sick leave, you should be in the office. This was the result of one too many complaints about Government workers who were on their RDOs. Dr. Clarke mandated that Army employees work five days a week, period. Later, and indirectly, I learned that Kyle considered my act of quitting to be that of a disloyal servant and that he had proclaimed "I would never work in this town again," so to speak, as a Government consultant for the Army directly or indirectly (to Kyle anyway). I also learned that the workforce had become, to put it quite bluntly, "scared shitless of Kyle." Apparently, the definition of disloyalty in Kyle's eyes had expanded to Army employees that took promotions and transferred over to work for the Navy. It also caused most Government employees pause when Kyle had a DoD contractor employee fired for disloyalty when a comment was casually made by them to someone else that the contract specialists really should have other priorities, like the programs they worked day in and out, ahead of the SPS task Kyle had deemed their top priority. Not to mention that taking time off at the end of the fiscal year was forbidden in writing for the first time ever. In the past, it had been unspoken and contract specialists just knew they shouldn't take time off at the end of the Government's fiscal year, and they didn't. Kyle was the first to put it in writing. Morale continued to plummet. At least two Army employees transferred to the Navy so they could get RDOs, several retired, and four actually moved to jobs in different states to escape Kyle's wrath. What they didn't know was Dr. Clarke had started listening to all the workforce rumors about Kyle's abuse of power. Kyle felt the need for speed; a speedy exit. There was no better way than to move on up into an even higher position in Government and Kyle had it all planned out. He was nominated to begin a career in the Senior Executive Service, just like Dr. Clarke, but first he'd have to go to Washington, DC for six months of extensive training. Then, the world was his oyster. Turns out, he was selected as the highest paid SES civilian in one of our top Contracting agencies recently. And guess what? Angel Baby took a higher paid position right under him. It was a sweet deal that Kyle would've never given to someone he was planning to hire, especially since the housing bubble hit beautiful central Florida like an excavation ball hits a building destined for destruction. He persuaded this top Contracting agency to not only buy his home, pay realtor commissions, moving costs, etc., but he also got them to do the same for Angel Baby. And just in the nick of time too. Angel Baby had one of those sub-prime mortgages on her Disney-like house in the development built on the toxic land of the former Navy base. I've also heard since Kyle left, Konstance didn't get the promotion she was hoping for; that went to Tim Bean, Angel Baby's gopher and Konstance was placed in a position where she could do the least amount to piss off the already disgruntled workforce.

THE DOD HOTLINE IS COLD AS ICE.

Within one week of taking the job involving the SPS, I knew I should've stuck to my original gut instinct to never have anything to do with it. But worse than my suspicions about how bad the functionality of SPS actually was, I found Konstance and Harley to be completely out of control and out of their league. I had no idea how little about contracting they both knew, until I delved deeper into the task at hand. Harley continuously gave me convoluted instructions to follow that I knew were not only not required by the Government contracting regulation, but wasteful and time-consuming. I protested. I persisted with my reasonable, logical rational recommendation for a cheaper, faster, smarter way to complete the task; first to Konstance and then to Angel Baby. I also stated in email that I could not continue to work for them, and I would quit, unless they took my recommendation. I even escalated it by sending an email only to Kyle, asking that he please listen to reason that Konstance and her right-hand man were just plain wrong and nothing they were saying was founded in regulation. I had an email back from Kyle saying I was right and he had advised Konstance to reach out to me right away, before it was too late. I actually believed him. Or, perhaps I grossly misunderstood him. Maybe there was more Tony Soprano speak in what he said in his email back to me than I even considered? Konstance then made it crystal clear to me that Angel Baby was in charge, and would make the ultimate decision, not Kyle. I now realize this was a test to see if Angel Baby could truly fly solo. No one ever returned my emails or phone calls, so I went back with one final email that said since I hadn't heard from them, I quit. I was on a time and materials labor hour contract anyway, so the Government had contracted to only pay me when they assigned work to me, and if they stopped assigning work, my contract would be over.

After I quit, I became obsessed with learning even more about the SPS. I searched the SPS Center of Excellence website to see if what I had been asked to do was required and found no answers. I then searched the internet and found two official DoD Inspector General (IG) Audit Reports which discussed in detail, the lack of functionality, user dissatisfaction among the contracting/contracts workforce and the waste of millions of the taxpayer's dollars. The Audit Report dated March 13, 2001, entitled "Standard Contracting System Use and User Satisfaction" is 75 pages long and contained a multitude of recommendations at the end that had never been responded to by the DoD Government officials responsible for the implementation of SPS within DoD. There was also a subsequent statement signed February 7, 2002 by the then Deputy Inspector General to the Subcommittee on National Security, Veterans Affairs and International Relations, House Committee on Government Reform on the SPS and the lack of response to the 2001 Audit Report. I felt relieved to read these reports and I decided to submit a written complaint to the DoD Hotline website, given in the Audit Reports. I used the on-line form found on the DoD Hotline website, relaying my very recent experience with SPS as justification for why SPS was still not working properly and wasting time and taxpayer's dollars. I also named names and mentioned that the Government instructions I'd been given on how I must use SPS were not in accordance with the

Defense Federal Acquisition Regulation. I questioned why the latest two DoD IG Audit Reports on the internet had remained unanswered. I requested a return email acknowledging receipt, which I never received.   Since I had never had an email response, I called the widely advertised DoD Hotline number (posters with the DoD Hotline telephone number and contact information are required to be placed in visible site at all DoD activities and DoD contractor's facilities) within two weeks of submitting my complaint and asked if it been received. I was simply told that it had been received and they were looking into it. Within a month, I received a phone call from a very mysterious sounding woman from the DoD Hotline, named Zeva, advising me that it was her responsibility to advise me that my complaint contained a lot of personal information that might be used against me and I should consider marking the entire complaint confidential. She went on to advise me, however, that if I marked it confidential, I must submit exactly the words she told me to write in an email to her attention. Then, she went on to advise me, they would have to redact it, and it would be virtually useless because there would little valuable information left. I was horrified to put it mildly. I asked her about the Whistleblower Protection Act among other things. I had a big decision to make. I decided that just because you're paranoid doesn't mean they aren't out to get you. I withdrew the complaint in its entirety by email the very same afternoon and asked that my email withdrawal be acknowledged by a return email. I never received a return email. I called several days later and asked the gentlemen who answered the phone if I could speak to Zeva. He said, "She's not in." I asked if I could leave her a message. He said, "Well, I can't tell you she'll call you back even if you leave her a message." He sounded stressed. I'm sure he was; I certainly was. Nevertheless, I left a message for her to please call me and acknowledge receipt of the withdrawal of my complaint. Before hanging up the phone, I asked the stressed-out man if he was a DoD contractor, or a civil servant. He said they were all civil servants in that office. Gee, now there's a surprise. I sent one last email to the mysterious woman requesting the courtesy of acknowledgement of the withdrawal of my complaint, since she had made such a big deal about the importance of *my* sending *her* an email her if I intended to mark it confidential or withdraw it. I've never heard from her or anyone at what I now call the DoD Iceline.

ALLIGATORS DON'T KNOW THEY'RE MONSTERS!

I'm not saying I'm smarter than a lot of people I worked with, and I know that some I worked with considered me a know-it-all. You see, what I called a great day was a day I'd legitimately win an argument with someone on the interpretation of a regulation. OK, I was a know-it-all (and still am). It was time for me to retire, and it is time to end this book. I was turning into The Shrew. Like I've said before, I'm not exactly the sympathetic/empathetic, touchy-feely type either. I tend to be a very opinionated, talkative, yet paranoid know-it-all who hates lazy and ignorant people. I've gotten a lot of lessons in my life that I needed, and then some, and believe me, I'm still learning every day. Did you know the Wizard of Oz (abbreviation for ounce) is an allegory about the gold-standard in the U.S.? I didn't until just the other day. And I thought it was a kid's movie!

However trite it may sound, the most important lesson I've learned is that your family, friends, dogs, and good health are the most important things in life, but it's also important to always do the best job you can and never be lazy on-the-clock. I've also learned that every experience, good or bad that you have is necessary; a rite of passage of sorts. That old saying, "If I knew then what I know now" is so true.

My mother died in 2006.. We spent a lot of time at a park on a lake, watching idiots feed the alligators. We fed the birds but only when no alligators were around. I attribute what I believe is a good (albeit biting) sense of humor to her. I remember one of the last things she said to me as I railed on at someone in the park who was feeding the alligators (the reason we have so many alligators attacks in Florida). She said, "No, they shouldn't feed them, but it's not the alligators fault; they don't know they're monsters." Reminds me of a lot of the people I met throughout my Federal Government career.

ABOUT THE AUTHOR

Ellen Roberge was born and raised in Florida, however, she worked as a Federal civil servant in Georgia, Hawaii, Virginia and Florida for 28 years before retiring in Florida. This is her first book.

16209673R00064

Made in the USA
Lexington, KY
10 July 2012